PRISONER OF CONSCIENCE

PRISONER
OF CONSCIENCE

One Man's Remarkable Journey from
Repression to Freedom

CHARLES YEATS

RIDER

LONDON · SYDNEY · AUCKLAND · JOHANNESBURG

1 3 5 7 9 10 8 6 4 2

First published in 2005 by Rider
an imprint of Ebury Press, Random House
20 Vauxhall Bridge Road, London SW1V 2SA

Random House Australia (Pty) Limited
20 Alfred Street, Milsons Point, Sydney
New South Wales 2061, Australia

Random House New Zealand Limited
18 Poland Road, Glenfield
Auckland 10, New Zealand

Random House South Africa (Pty) Limited
Endulini, 5A Jubilee Road
Parktown 2193, South Africa

Random House UK Limited Reg. No. 954009

Papers used by Rider
are natural recyclable products made from wood
grown in sustainable forests.

Typeset by SX Composing DTP, Rayleigh, Essex
Printed and bound in Great Britain
by Mackays of Chatham plc, Kent

A CIP catalogue record for this book is available
from the British Library

ISBN: 1-84604001-9

For Alison

CONTENTS

Foreword by Archbishop Desmond ...

Preface by Charles Yeats

CONTENTS

FOREWORD
BY DESMOND TUTU
ARCHBISHOP EMERITUS

Charles tells me that he owns a salt and pepper set consisting of a four-inch model of the Afrikaner White supremacist Eugene Terreblanche and another of me, Desmond. Terreblanche is of course salt to my pepper! The existence of this twisted bit of anarchic art is highly amusing and it reminds me of how we used to laugh, and how we cried, at the stupidity of apartheid, with its impossible vision of a pure White state in Africa.

Charles' book reminded me of the laughter and the crying. It includes a very readable account of apartheid written from the perspective of a privileged White South African, whose Christian discipleship forced him to take an uncomfortable choice that led into a journey of self-discovery and a continuing search for truth and meaning in a world that defies anyone to hold consistently to their ideals.

The road he took is a fascinating one, and I hugely enjoyed how it starts with his tongue-in-cheek description of first encounters at Harrow School and how he cleverly weaves a love story into the narrative. England is also a good place to start the book because we tend to forget that the British have a particular responsibility for the suffering of my people. Not only did they practise apartheid throughout Africa long before the Afrikaner but also their empire mercilessly subjugated the whole of Southern Africa in the nineteenth century with the principal aim of exploiting its mineral wealth.

Charles' account of his trial is a touch too understated. It did, after all, involve not one but two Archbishops! Although I was not directly involved myself, I know that it helped raise the issue of conscientious objection to military service, which we Blacks did not regard as a matter of conscience at all, to a higher level. We greatly appreciated what he and his fellow conscientious objectors did because by saying that apartheid was indefensible and by enduring imprisonment for their beliefs they were saying that we mattered.

I was intrigued to discover from the book what happened to Charles after his release from prison, and how his interest and ongoing work in Business Ethics was sparked by the contribution Big Business made both to sustaining apartheid and then to ending it when apartheid no longer paid. I well remember how we attempted to challenge corporate power by the campaign for economic sanctions, and how the withdrawal of large foreign companies, such as Barclays, helped tip the balance of power away from the apartheid regime. It is good to know that Charles and others are continuing this engagement.

Charles' response to the 'war on terror' also helpfully reminded me of how all our lives are bounded by the reality of empire, with its ruthless control over strategic resources owned by other nations, and of how the beneficiaries of empire should not lose sight of this when judging whether a particular war is just. He wisely does not venture to offer solutions to the conflict in the Middle East but instead recalls how Nelson Mandela and his fellow African National Congress guerrillas were demonised and hunted down as terrorists, and how the conflict in South Africa looked equally intractable.

As a fellow pilgrim, I was also intrigued to read where Charles has ventured on his Christian journey. It is clear from his response to fundamentalist religion and to the schism threatened by the issue of homosexuality in the Anglican Church that he has moved a long way, while struggling to hold on to his roots. Not every one will agree with the positions he takes. However, I believe we all need to heed his call to love and friendship, because there is no other way forward.

PREFACE

The decision to write this book was taken after a visit to Ground Zero in New York and the still damaged Pentagon in Washington, DC on a project engaged with combating terrorist finance and money-laundering. I was prevented from continuing further down the eastern seaboard of the United States by a series of 'twisters' flattening everything in their path. To escape them, I bunkered down in the Shenandoah National Park, close to the Civil War battlefields. The television news carried the latest reports from the war in Iraq, which was already provoking fears of another Vietnam. Back home in Britain, a senior intelligence officer announced that a terrorist attack on London, possibly using a weapon of mass destruction, was 'inevitable'. With all this din of war about me, and with some time on my hands, it occurred to me that I had a story to tell about love and friendship.

I have also tried to tell the story of apartheid for a new generation that does not understand what the word means. While all know that Nelson Mandela was imprisoned on Robben Island for twenty-seven years, many will express surprise when told that apartheid society was one where Black and White people were forced to live apart and were not permitted to attend the same schools. Lest we forget, I have written a short personalised account of this African holocaust, which I particularly hope will be read by young people exploring the evil of racialism. I also hope it will be read by the increasing number of visitors flocking to the sunny skies, beaches and game reserves of the new South Africa. It would be a pity were they to remain ignorant of the tragic human drama that took place.

Of my friends and supporters, to whom I owe this book, I

have a particular debt of gratitude to Amnesty International, which adopted me as a Prisoner of Conscience when I was imprisoned for refusing to defend apartheid and mobilised its global network on my behalf. Sadly, the thousands of letters sent to me in prison were withheld until my release and the task of replying to each one then was too great. I hope this book will make up for my failure to write a personal thank you, and will be read as a tribute to all those who kept me from the killing fields of Southern Africa and helped me survive Detention Barracks and Pretoria Central Prison.

I also wish to thank my family. They have patiently listened to me read each chapter as it has come off the word processor. Some parts have met with loud disapproval, especially those passages where I have described them in less than flattering terms. My two teenage children have also been embarrassed to hear me relate some of the more intimate moments of their parents' courtship. I have occasionally been ordered to rewrite. Thanks to them, you only get to read the censored version.

Charles Yeats

MAP OF SOUTHERN AFRICA

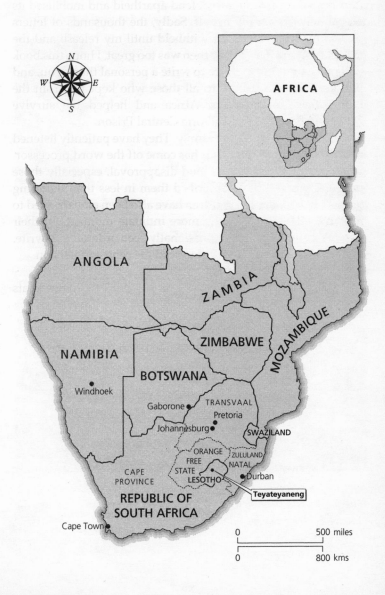

During my imprisonment, I relived my favourite run of all, on the famous Robberg beach . . . (p. 111)

1

HARROW SCHOOL

> This could well have been the best XV that Harrow have ever
> produced since they took up rugby football in 1928.
>
> (*Country Life*, 9 January 1975)

To be a White South African under apartheid was to be favoured in every way. One measure of how privileged I was is that, after attending the finest school in South Africa, I finished my schooling by spending a term at the famous English public school Harrow.

My first impressions were of a rather grubby set of buildings dotted along a busy high street in a grey London suburb. I was assigned to Westacre, an old, cramped and rather dilapidated house, furthest from the centre of the school. No sooner had I stowed my belongings in my damp and musty smelling room, than, to my horror, a new boy knocked timidly on the door and announced that he was my fag. After thanking him kindly and explaining that I did not think I would have need of his services, I let him go. After all the parents had deposited their sons and had left, the house started to reverberate with brutish shouts of 'BOY!', followed by the stampeding sounds of small boys on the stairs scrambling to do the caller's bidding.

The hubbub on the stairs did not let up until we were

summoned to the oak-panelled house dining room for tea. This led to my first encounter with the English public schoolboy. It was not a comfortable experience. I was made acutely aware of my South African accent. The genteel banter passed over my head and made me feel every inch the country bumpkin I was. I discovered that the art of elegant conversation was never to say anything serious. To express an opinion was in the worst taste. I was also floored when asked, quite openly, how many times a week I masturbated. I recall looking at the boy in disbelief and being struck dumb, not so much in embarrassment but by the sheer brazenness of the question. Nothing in all my ten years at an all-male boarding school had prepared me for such a personal and very public interrogation. I decided that all I had heard about the English public schoolboy was true and that I had better watch out for myself.

By way of contrast, Hilton College, the school I had just left in South Africa, was an altogether more wholesome and really very grand place. It is set in splendid isolation on an estate of ten thousand acres in the Natal Midlands. The school is approached along an avenue of tall plane trees, with a stone-built chapel at its end. The distinctive Cape Dutch-style of architecture, with its imposing white gabled fronts, has been maintained in the design of all the main buildings. Each house stands in its own spacious formal gardens. The educational facilities boast a modern library and theatre complex superior to most civic ones. The abundant playing fields, tennis and squash courts, gymnasium and Olympic-size swimming pool provide for most kinds of sport. An American visitor I once showed round exclaimed in admiration, 'Gee, but this is Harvard.'

Hilton had also abolished barbarisms such as fagging and flogging long before my time. There was even a separate house for new boys, which provided for their gradual integration into boarding-school life and protected them from the bullying and abuse common in an all-male establishment. Although adolescence was a problem, I was not particularly aware of an atmosphere of desperately repressed sexuality. The compulsory sport and vigorous outdoor pursuits took care of that side of life. Even on Sundays there was no time to be idle because there was the vast estate to explore, with the rushing torrent of the Tugela River to swim in. Even dressed in my boater and tails at Harrow, I could be excused for thinking that I had stepped down in the world.

My Hilton Headmaster, Raymond Slater, had conceived the idea of an exchange with Harrow. As I had been brought up in Basutoland, the tiny landlocked kingdom in the middle of South Africa and then a remote part of Britain's African Empire, he thought it important for me to widen my horizons by exploring the mother country. I suspect he also had a rather soft spot for the Basutoland Yeats. We were a modest family of traders from one of the poorest countries in the world, and he knew that, unlike the majority of boys who came from affluent families in Johannesburg and Durban, it cost my parents to send their three sons to his expensive boarding school. I rather think that he took satisfaction at the thought that he was making it possible for one of my family to go on to one of the most prestigious and expensive schools in the world.

At eighteen, with all the self-confidence of a boy at the top of his school, I was ripe for the adventure. I had never left the borders of South Africa and had never flown in an aeroplane. I was off to see the Queen. Her photograph stood proudly in my grandparents' living room alongside the citations for the Member of the Order of the British Empire (MBE), awarded to my grandmother Joy, and the Officer of the Order of the British Empire (OBE) awarded to my grandfather Charles, for services rendered to the BaSotho nation. I can still recall the excitement of flying low into London and trying to see whether I could make out Buckingham Palace from all the tall buildings rushing past.

My term at Harrow was spent doing what I did best: playing games. I ended up playing for an unbeaten school rugby team, the first for forty years. I captained Westacre to

3

victory in the keenly contested inter-house competition. I was also chosen to play for the renowned Harlequins' club in an English Schools' Under 19 XV against the University of Paris. This match taught me something about the ancient rivalry between the English and the French because it was played with such savagery that I barely survived to explore Paris and its celebrated nightlife. My housemaster, who idolised rugby as much as any South African, was immensely pleased with these sporting achievements. He took a young master and me to the Oxford and Cambridge match at Twickenham as a reward. We had to stop the car on the way back to let the young teacher, who had celebrated Oxford's win with a little too much enthusiasm, be violently sick.

Instead of being left alone at school for half-term, I was kindly invited to North Yorkshire by one of my new friends at Westacre, who promised to take me out hunting, the ultimate test of horsemanship. The day we spent with the Zetland hunt was one of the most thrilling of my life. He mounted me on his father's largest hunter, Mush, a magnificent animal, who was at least two or three hands taller than any horse I had ridden before. Mush danced every step of the way, kept his ears pricked forward for the sound of the horn, and was ready for the chase. It was as much as I could do to stop him overtaking the Master of the Hunt and he effortlessly took me over one hedge so high that I shut my eyes. I escaped blooding because the only fox we saw, with the hounds hot on his heels, led them into a cover, doubled back on his tracks and left the pack baying their fury.

All this sport might have been the educational value of this term for me. However, to give these institutions their due, it is impossible to pass through an English public school without something of real value rubbing off along the way. On the academic front, an enthusiastic master introduced me to the subject of economics, which ever since I have found an invaluable tool for understanding how the world works. Another young master, later a Tory MP, gave me a taste of

British parliamentary life by taking me to a dinner in the House of Commons, where he set me up to ask a question on Britain's naval base in South Africa at Simonstown. The Dramatics Society put on an excellent performance of Robert Bolt's play *The Mission*, with its example of a group of Jesuit missionaries in South America defying colonial and ecclesiastical power, which challenged me to think harder about social justice in South Africa. There was a thriving Christian society and chapel, where I was encouraged in the Christian faith.

I was also fortunate to attend Harrow in the term when 'Churchill Songs' was first held in the Royal Albert Hall, with Winston Churchill's widow, Clemmie, in attendance. This annual concert was held in honour of Harrow's greatest old boy and least promising pupil, who was famously threatened by his father with a career in business because his teachers reported he would never merit a commission in the army. Of all his exploits, including those as a war correspondent in the Boer War, the story that I most enjoyed was the one of his entrance examination in which the young Winston tells how he put his name at the top of the paper and then could not find another word to write. As I was never very successful at examinations myself, I was greatly heartened by this story and made a special visit to the Fourth Form room to see where he had carved his name on a wooden desk. In this shrine to the great man, I resolved to try to be more of an individual.

My final noteworthy experience while in England was of Oxford. James and Peter Baron, twins in the Harrow rugby team, encouraged me to attend the public schools' Christian conference held annually between Christmas and New Year at Wycliffe Hall, a Church of England theological college. In between lectures by eminent theologians, who I recall being oddly burdened with defending a faith I had never seriously questioned, I managed to visit some of the colleges and student haunts. This started to focus my mind on my own looming university education and, on the strength of my new academic interest, I decided to major in economics. I left Oxford wistfully, never dreaming that one day I would return as a member of the university.

From Oxford, I flew home via Rome, where I spent a night in the Vatican City. If the Christian heritage of Britain impressed me, that of Rome awed me. I remember wandering about on the steps of St Peter's thinking just how provincial the church in South Africa must be to the Pope and his Curia. From this historical and international vantage point, the claims of the Church of England also looked terribly pretentious and I had my first doubts about my membership of the so-called worldwide Anglican Communion. I visited all the right places, such as the Sistine Chapel, but was unable to take in much of the detail because I was too enthralled by the story of the Church. What I was unable to decide was whether the magnificence of the Vatican represented a betrayal or vindication of the Galilean Jesus and his followers, some of whom had met their end in the nearby Colosseum. This appreciation of the ambiguity of the Church has dogged me ever since, never allowing me to enter too wholeheartedly into its institutional life, with the result that there has been a side of me looking in from the outside not really wanting to be a part of it.

Rome completed my first-ever tour outside the borders of South Africa and marked the end of my finishing school. I arrived back just in time to start the new academic year at the University of Natal, at its campus in Durban, South Africa's second city and busiest port. I was able to lodge with my parents in their new beachfront home in the Durban suburb of La Lucia, which they had recently bought after our family business in Basutoland was taken over by a large South African firm headquartered in Durban and which appointed my father a director. Living so close to the sea was a novel experience and I started each day with a ritual run on the beach followed by a refreshing swim.

My undergraduate degree also provided the opportunity to play yet more serious sport. I took up what in England is the sport of kings but what in South Africa is the sport of the

farmer, polo. In colonial Basutoland anyone of any consequence would have had to play polo and my father rose to
captain the Orange Free State and Basutoland Polo Team. I
now joined him at the Inanda Polo Club, set in the midst of
sugar-cane fields outside Durban, where we stabled our horses
and played with a motley crew of farmers. Nearby was the
Phoenix Settlement, the first ashram set up by the young
Mahatma Gandhi, the liberator of India, who honed his
political skills by first opposing racism in South Africa and
whose community was dedicated to the exploration of a simple
lifestyle, non-violence and non-racialism.

I was dimly aware at the time that my contrasting lifestyle
was not sustainable. Black opposition to White privilege had
whittled away at the system of apartheid, increasingly making
us aware just how unjustifiable our privileges were. The lid on
the pressure cooker could not be kept on indefinitely and great
hisses of steam kept on bursting out. Then, in my second year
as an undergraduate, Soweto, the Black township outside
Johannesburg, erupted on 16 June 1976. The schoolchildren
took matters into their own hands. They rejected Bantu education, designed to prepare them only for menial positions
within apartheid society. They confronted the police and the
army and were shot. It was the turning point for my
generation. It was now impossible to sit comfortably in university lecture halls, from which Black students were excluded
and required to attend their own racially segregated and much
inferior universities. We were suddenly very much aware that
the institution we belonged to was the exact antithesis of a
university. Afterwards, even when galloping at full tilt down a
polo ground, I could not escape the guilt.

My comfortable lifestyle also had to end because the main-
tenance of White supremacy depended on a conscript army.
This meant that every White male was called up for military
service and was required to serve a period of two years in one
of the three branches of the South African Defence Force
(SADF). There was no provision of a non-military alternative

form of national service for conscientious objectors. Any person refusing to undergo military training was therefore liable to be tried before a court martial and sentenced to a term in a military prison or detention barracks (DB) – an as yet untested option. The best one could do was to defer military service for as long as possible, as I did, by enrolling after school for a university degree. A further deferral for a post-graduate degree was rarely allowed.

While I unquestioningly accepted many aspects of life in apartheid South Africa, I had at least expressed my unease about military service when this irksome reality was first thrust upon me at the age of sixteen. This was the age when all White boys were registered at school as members of the SADF. Without advance warning, we were herded into the school hall, briefly addressed by an army officer and required to sign up, from which moment we were legally bound to obey any call-up until the age of sixty-five. I signed in a state of fear and confusion like all the rest. But after the military had left I plucked up the courage to complain to our Headmaster that I did not think it right to kill in defence of apartheid and objected to the way we had been given no choice about our registration. Raymond Slater responded with his blunt integrity that he did not care for it either but the state gave him no choice in the matter.

Raymond had done his best to support me in the years since I had left Hilton and, with my call-up looming the month after my undergraduate finals, he was the confidant I turned to. When I repeated the concerns I had raised at school about military service, he arranged for me to meet the Roman Catholic Archbishop of Durban, Denis Hurley, an uncompromising opponent of apartheid, who had publicly upheld the right to refuse military service in the SADF on the grounds of conscience.

Archbishop Hurley was born in a lighthouse. The story goes that the light so infused his conception that he was born to shine. He was consecrated in 1947, at the remarkably young age of thirty-one, as the first South African-born bishop in the Catholic Church. He was later to play a leading role at the Second Vatican Council and served in many secular roles, including those of President of the South African Institute of Race Relations and Chancellor of the University of Natal. One indication of the stature of his Christian leadership was that my headmaster, a Presbyterian, sent me, an Anglican, to him for counselling. He was truly a bishop for all.

He was quite clear in the counsel he gave me that the Christian tradition expects a follower of Christ to follow his conscience in the matter of military service. I do not recall him adding that apartheid was indefensible, but that was not necessary because it was clear from all he stood for. This unvarnished truth was delivered with a gentle understanding and compassion for what I was going through. Although setting before me a hard road, in the silent conspiracy all about me, where few church leaders dared to denounce military service publicly, what he said came as a huge relief because it confirmed for me the truth I had worked out for myself. Our meeting was the start of something close to hero worship for me. I recall feeling such love for the man that it was as if he was my father.

I was not yet ready though to follow where my conscience was leading me. My public school education had instilled in me a good deal of all that is best in this tradition but it had woefully prepared me for any role other than being one of the officer class. At this stage of my personal development it was therefore virtually impossible for me to play the dissident; I was programmed to aspire to high office. As soon as my degree results were published, I applied for a further deferment of military service to begin what was then regarded as the fast track to senior executive status and its rewards, an MBA in Finance at the University of Witwatersrand's Graduate School of Business. Permission was granted and I moved, in 1978, to Igoli, the City of Gold, the African name for Johannesburg. In exchange for house master duties, I took up free lodgings at the prestigious Anglican school of St John's in the leafy suburb of Houghton, a safe distance from the boiling Black townships of Soweto, Alexandra and Sharpeville.

My life in the business hub of South Africa passed pleasantly enough. The newly appointed Director of the Business School, Gideon Jacobs, a respected former opposition politician, succeeded in attracting a broad range of outside speakers to make the course both interesting and international in scope. One visiting speaker, Simon Brand, the Deputy Governor of the Reserve Bank, South Africa's central bank, made a deep impression on me by presenting a chillingly honest account of the economic and social crisis facing the country posed by the rapidly expanding Black population. He made it clear that, without substantial foreign investment, population growth would outstrip the ability of the economy to generate the jobs needed to promote social cohesion. In the context of political instability, international sanctions and a growing flight of capital, the implications hardly needed spelling out.

In response to this lecture, and after receiving a fresh set of call-up papers, I thought, as I was a member of the officer class, the state would not want to jail me and would accept an offer to serve in one of South Africa's economic development corporations as an alternative to military service. I wrote to the Exemption Board and proposed this alternative and explained that job creation was vital for peace. I also pointed out that an economic development corporation would use my training in economics and finance, which would otherwise be wasted. The response was entirely predictable. Doubtless fearing an avalanche of conscripts applying for a similar exemption, the Exemption Board replied that there was no provision in the law for a non-military form of national service. The letter went on to insist that all South Africans had a duty to defend their country from the onslaught of Communist and anti-Christian forces on our borders.

With only one more term of the MBA programme to go, I

considered the option of simply failing to turn up for my call-up. I thought it might be possible to hide in the rabbit warren of Hillbrow, the Soho of Johannesburg, where it would be virtually impossible for the military police to find me. With this in mind, and wanting to do something positive at the same time, I contacted the South African Council of Churches (SACC), whose offices were close to Hillbrow, to investigate whether the Council had work for me. To my surprise, I received an immediate reply asking me to meet with Bishop Desmond Tutu, then the General Secretary of the SACC.

Desmond Tutu was, if anything, an even more embattled bishop than Archbishop Hurley at this time. He had only recently taken over at the Council and his predecessor John Rees had left him an awful mess. A large sum of money donated by overseas supporters had gone missing. While few doubted the integrity of John Rees, who, it was widely assumed, had passed the money on to the enemies of the state and therefore could not publicly account for where the money had gone, the Bureau for State Security, aptly named BOSS, was determined to use the unaccounted for funds to discredit the SACC and, in particular, Bishop Tutu. Although what was expected of me was never spelt out, I suspected Bishop Tutu hoped that I would be able to sort out the tangled web of accounts and help him prepare his defence.

A brief walking tour of the Council's offices, however, persuaded me that taking on its chaotic administration was way beyond my powers and my years. For one thing, the complexity involved demanded a professional accountant, with considerable experience. For another, most of the staff were Black and would have resented and possibly resisted any hard decisions I might have proposed. With BOSS busy digging away to find any sign of dirt, it would also have been impossible for me to fade into the background and hide the fact that I was a draft dodger; even a humble backroom role at the SACC was simply far too exposed. I was forced to accept that, even if I had the courage to disobey my call-up, I could not take on the job.

In an increasing state of anxiety, I retreated for the Easter holidays to my grandparents' home in the small village of Teyateyaneng in neighbouring Lesotho, the landlocked kingdom in the middle of South Africa where I had grown up. Despite all the changes taking place around them since Britain had granted Basutoland independence in 1966, they had resolutely maintained the leisurely colonial way of life of this former British protectorate. I always found it a secure and tranquil haven, conducive to thinking things through, and escaped there as often as I could. There was also something very comforting about being in the familiar surroundings I had known since childhood.

But not even the gentle ministrations of my grandparents and their wonderful old house servants could soothe my mental strain. Hoping that I would receive a divine revelation as to what I should do next, I took myself off to attend the traditional three-hour service of readings and meditations on Good Friday at the small African monastery of Masite. This collection of humble BaSotho huts was then the ı idquarters in Lesotho of the Society of the Sacred Mission (SSM), the order of Anglican priests who ran the mission outside Teyateyaneng. The three long hours were an agony because the only light in the small chapel shone on the crucifix hung over the altar.

Back in my grandparents' home, I spent more hours alone on my knees. I knew of no one else who had refused or was wrestling with refusing military service. My parents were opposed and I dared not raise the subject with my grandfather, who had fought in a South African regiment in the First World War and whose tin hat and medals were proudly displayed in a cabinet in his living room. In my misery and isolation, my thinking and prayers kept coming back to the inside of a prison, something which neither my background nor my education had remotely prepared me for. Eventually, with my mind growing heavier and heavier until I could no longer think straight, I gave in and accepted that I lacked the courage either to go through with a trial or to become a fugitive in South

Africa and so would simply have to leave the country.

Up to this point, I had resolutely resisted this choice. Like many of my generation, I had fallen under the influence of a group of White political and religious leaders who encouraged us to see our futures in South Africa come what may. At a time when many were emigrating, we were exhorted to stay and to play a part in helping bring about a peaceful end to apartheid. Prominent among them was South Africa's Billy Graham, the Anglican evangelist Michael Cassidy, who wrote a book at the time with the title *Prisoners of Hope* and another with the subtitle *A South African Pilgrimage in the Politics of Love*. I now found myself resenting their failure to confront the state over the major obstacles to my generation staying on in South Africa, such as military service. I rather bitterly decided that their brand of well meaning evangelicalism was full of text but short of context.

Nevertheless, with my mind made up that there was no option but to leave, I was wracked with guilt. I resolved to do all in my power to keep open the possibility of returning by badgering the SADF from abroad for permission to perform a non-military form of national service. Armed with this decision, back in Johannesburg after my holiday, I lost no time in approaching Deloittes, one of the international accounting firms with offices in Johannesburg and applied and was accepted for a trainee post in London. My plan now was to acquire the accounting skills my brief exposure to the chaos at the SACC had convinced me were essential for managing a large complex organisation.

With only weeks to go before my call-up in July 1979, I completed the MBA and then boarded a plane for Heathrow. I took off wondering whether I would ever return and with a sense of having 'jumped ship'. My feelings of loss and guilt were so strong that no sooner had I settled into my new lodgings in London House, a residence for Commonwealth students in Mecklenburgh Square, Holborn, than I wrote and informed the Exemption Board of my whereabouts and that I

13

would be studying for the chartered accountancy qualification in the hope that this would keep me on the right side of the law. To my relief, I received a terse reply extending my deferment and requesting me to inform the SADF on my return to South Africa.

With the SADF off my back for the time being, I reckoned that I deserved a complete rest from South Africa after the nerve-racking past few months and set out to enjoy London. I resolved to have nothing to do with the anti-apartheid movement, at least for the time being, and to avoid exiled South Africans. I started each working day by walking from London House to my new offices near St Paul's Cathedral. In my lunchtime breaks, I took to buying a sandwich and eating it on the Embankment, from where I would admire the Thames and the London skyline. I tried not to think about how much of the wealth on display in London's fine buildings was owed the miners toiling miles under the city, Igoli, I had just left. It was wonderful to walk anonymously in the safe, relaxed and happy London crowd.

One Saturday, I took myself off on a nostalgic visit to watch a rugby match at Harrow. There I met James Baron, the captain of our unbeaten Harrow XV, who, after graduating from Cambridge, had been invited back on to the school staff as a mathematics master. He alerted his raffish twin, Peter, who was taking his teacher's qualification in London, that I had arrived in the big smoke and could do with some company. Peter took me under his wing and invited me to join a Bible study group, which met weekly after work at the church of St Helen's, Bishopsgate, in the heart of the City, the financial centre. He was not to know how much this was to change my life.

My first memories of Alison are of a colourful and noisy distraction. She was a medical student, studying at St Bartholomew's Medical College (Bart's), who would arrive breathless and just in time for Bible study on her ancient bicycle, Gertrude, which she rode all over London. While the rest of us got down to serious study, she tended to lark about. Although she appeared to know the Bible better than the rest of us and kept copious notes of all the talks the earnest young curate gave, one could not help thinking that, in a different setting, she might be something of a subversive. Whenever our group was called upon to cook the evening meal, she was sure to be in the thick of the action and could be quite bossy, certainly in her treatment of me. She was also impossible to ignore on account of her hair. This is a shade of red with all the deep colours of autumn mixed up in it. An auctioneer once singled her out in the crowd and described it as Titian. When it caught my eye, I thought St Paul, who wrote of a woman's hair as her crowning glory, would understand the attraction.

It would be a mistake to describe Alison at this time as being flirtatious. Anything suggestive of that would have been frowned upon at St Helen's, with its strong evangelical tradition and volatile mix of young students, nurses, secretaries and bold unattached City gents, like myself. Young people were encouraged to keep a wide circle of friends and to dedicate all their spare time to evangelism. The view on relationships was that they got in the way, and was best summed up in the advice to 'keep a foot apart'. This made for a slightly electric atmosphere whenever we were allowed to put down our Bibles and socialise. The tension was exacerbated by the example of the church's two single male clergy and their preaching, with its frequent polemical broadsides against Roman Catholics, liberal Anglicans and gays.

However, Alison, with all her Viking blood, was not easily cowed. She invited me to the flat above a betting shop in Bride Street, Islington, where she cooked South African bobotie. She maintains that it was her flatmates who provided me with a ticket to watch her, in Bart's production of *Pygmalion*, play the part of Mrs Higgins, a character that strongly reminded me of my grandmother. She showed a clear preference for being seated next to me at our Bible study meetings. On the pretext that I spoke too quietly, she managed to sit uncomfortably close to me in the back seat of Peter's car. I was invited to meet her rather forbidding parents. To my shame, I reciprocated none of this attention, partly because I too regarded relationships at the time as something that should wait, but more importantly because, when we met, I was on the verge of returning to South Africa and I did not want to complicate matters by leaving an attachment behind.

Despite putting on a brave face to my new friends, the truth was that I could not shake off a sense of failure and the self-knowledge that, if I remained much longer in Britain, it would be impossible to return. What was difficult to deny was that my immediate Christian task was in South Africa and not in London. This understanding had been shaped by years of Christian formation, starting with the SSM fathers at Teyateyaneng, who had made no distinction between White and Black and loved and served both with a devotion that was infectious. The process had continued at school, where I read about the lives of a succession of prophetic Christian leaders in South Africa, such as the Nobel Laureate and President of the African National Congress, Chief Albert Luthuli, the radical churchman and author of *Naught for your Comfort*, Father Trevor Huddleston, and the great liberal Alan Paton, who wrote *Cry the Beloved Country*. All these had left me in no doubt that apartheid was especially offensive to the Christian Gospel and not only was it indefensible but it should be actively opposed.

I had also made a mistake in fleeing to London because the British media would not let me off the hook. The extensive reporting of South African affairs kept the evil of apartheid ever before me. Furthermore, the power of the visual image, denied me in South Africa, where television had only recently been introduced, ensured that the nightmare of all that was happening back home was a constant torment. Excellent BBC documentaries also helped me better understand grand apartheid, with its impossible vision of separate but equal territories for each of South Africa's population groups. For the first time I saw the hopelessly overcrowded and over-grazed dumping grounds where people were deserted on a barren plot with little more than a tent and a latrine hole. It is a terrible personal indictment that I only fully grasped the extent of grand apartheid and of South Africa's military and economic destabilisation of the whole Southern African region from abroad.

The media also brought to my attention the trials and imprisonment of two cousins, Peter Moll and Richard Steele, for refusing military service in the SADF. They were members of the Baptist Church and the first to publicly refuse conscription in South Africa. They had each been sentenced to a year in detention barracks and had been subjected to repeated bouts of solitary confinement for refusing to wear military uniform. Their courageous public stand heightened my sense of guilt at being at large, when I too might be showing the same kind of leadership in South Africa. More than that, by displaying that rare bravery to go where no one has gone before, they blazed a path for less courageous people to follow.

Tugging at me in the opposite direction was the lure of the City. It was the obvious next career move. I had also recently met a South African Christian and banker, Ken Costa, now a 'big hitter' in the City, who presented a possible role model. He worked for Warburgs in the exciting field of mergers and acquisitions. A colleague at one of his drinks parties suggested that I should apply to join the bank. Fortunately at the time Ken lived in a modest apartment and drove such a battered old car that he was a very poor advertisement for merchant banking. The City was also not as glamorous a place then as it was to become later on in the eighties, when it started to buzz with young upwardly mobile professionals or Yuppies, with their designer clothing and BMW sports cars.

A stronger pull was the Church. London presented a fascinating range of churches. In contrast to St Helen's, with its

perfunctory worship and Dick Lucas's long expository sermons,
there was Ken's much more lively church, Holy Trinity
Brompton (HTB). At Ken's invitation, I attended a service and
took with me another South African friend, who was totally
unchurched and something of a *femme fatale*. To my surprise,
she came out a Christian, impressing on me HTB's amazing
powers of evangelism. With many of the foreign students in
London, I regularly attended All Souls, Langham Place, with
its famous preacher John Stott, who supporters told me was the
unofficial evangelical Archbishop of Canterbury. I also
attended the University Church of Christ the King, where I
found the beautiful old liturgy I had been brought up with in
Basutoland. With all these spiritual influences, I felt the
stirrings of what would later be described to me as a vocation.

The strongest siren of them all though was Alison. She had
clearly come to intrude on my thoughts for the future because,
years later, my aunt and uncle reminded me of a visit to their
home in Henley-on-Thames at the time when I confided that I
had met a girl with red hair whom I hoped one day to marry.
And of all my new friends in London, I chose Alison to help me
celebrate my birthday. After dinner at the Black Sheep, near
Coram Fields, as every well-brought up South African would
do, I escorted her back to Bride Street. Outside the door of her
flat, she invited me in for coffee and coyly mentioned that her
two flatmates were out. This presented the first and only
opportunity we had to be alone together. It was one of those
moments when a decision one way or the other might place
one on an irrevocable path. Perhaps it was standing in Bride
Street that flashed this warning. I turned and fled.

Pulled one way and then the other, I was something of a
wreck by Christmas, and would have spent New Year mop-
ing on my own had Peter Baron not insisted that I attend the
St Helen's New Year house party at Fairmile Court. While all
had a good time, I spent much of it alone with my troubled
conscience. As a companion, I picked out of the library *Letters
and Papers from Prison*, a compilation of the writings of the

German Protestant theologian Dietrich Bonhoeffer, who was executed by the Nazis in the closing days of the Second World War for his part in a plot to assassinate Hitler. The choice of this book suggests that my mind was all but made up. His letters moved me by revealing a man who had finally discovered a sense of freedom in prison from an evil and shameful society of which, like me, he was an unwilling member.

Still I prevaricated. I worried that if I returned to challenge the might of the SADF it would be seen as a foolish tilting at windmills. I knew that many of my evangelical Christian friends would judge me for not submitting to the divine authority of the state. But what weighed even heavier was the warning in those words of Sir Francis Drake: 'it is not the beginning, but the continuing of the same until it be thoroughly finished'. With my stock of courage wholly untested, what I most feared was that my initial defiance would end in a whimper when the going got rough.

The ticking of the clock towards the New Year helped bring an end to this agony of guilt and self-doubt. I had given myself until the end of the year to settle in London, and had promised myself that I would not go into the New Year without a decision one way or the other. Therefore, shortly before we were due to file outside to sing 'Auld Lang Syne' on the moonlit lawn of Fairmile Court, I roused my pathetically limp and self-indulgent mind and forced myself to decide.

I decided that I had to return to South Africa, even if it meant risking failure, because I could no longer bear the unhappiness and guilt of living in London. With the decision behind me, I sang in the New Year and then madly joined in the Scottish dances on the frosty lawn.

My last night in England was spent at a dinner party at Peter's lodgings to celebrate the leap year, 29 February 1980. For those unfamiliar with the tradition, this is the day that women are entitled to ask a man to marry them. The theme, chosen by the five girls who each anonymously invited a partner, was Rudolf Rassendyll, the romantic hero of the gripping yarn by Anthony Hope, *The Prisoner of Zenda*. Peter borrowed a black tie for me and insisted that I wear it for the occasion. As I had not worn this evening dress before and associated it with the film role of James Bond, I remember feeling hugely self-conscious. Alison, sitting by my side, said I looked especially fetching in it.

We partied into the early hours, when the combination of wine and good company must have gone to my head, for I committed my first indiscretion in my relationship with Alison. When the elaborate menus were circulated for signing, I relaxed my guard and added the first line of the poem by Robert Burns 'My love is like a red, red rose' after my signature. I sobered up immediately, instantly recognising what I had done. Fortunately, the party then quickly broke up and, desperate not to become emotionally entangled at this last moment, I declined Alison's offer to see me off at the airport for my early morning flight. All the way to Heathrow on the tube, I cursed myself for having been so reckless with a girl I had only known for three months. I hoped and prayed she would not find the time to read the full poem:

> *My love is like a red, red rose*
> *That's newly sprung in June:*
> *My love is like the melody*
> *That's sweetly played in tune.*
>
> *As fair art thou, my bonnie lass,*
> *So deep in love am I:*
> *And I will love thee still, my dear,*
> *Till a' the seas gang dry.*
>
> *Till a' the seas gang dry, my dear,*
> *And the rocks melt wi' the sun:*
> *And I will love thee still, my dear,*
> *While the sands o' life shall run.*

And fare thee weel, my only love,
And fare thee weel a while!
And I will come again, my love,
Thou' it were ten thousand mile.

2

THE ZULU

He told them too of the sickness of the land, and of how the grass
had disappeared, and of the dongas that ran from hill to valley, and
valley to hill; how it was a land of old men and women, and mothers
and children; how the maize grew barely to the height of a man; how
the tribe was broken, the house was broken, and the man broken;
how when they went away, many never came back, many never
wrote any more.

(Alan Paton, *Cry the Beloved Country*)

The most painful part of living through the closing years of
apartheid was to see and experience how it scarred the land
and people of Southern Africa – for both are very beautiful. As
I watched the land from the window of the plane bringing me
back from London and anticipated meeting my family and
friends, I was filled with conflicting emotions. One part of me
felt very old, worn out and angry that apartheid had stolen
away my youth and that of many others. But another part
could not suppress a sense of pride and rejoicing in my
country. Stretched out far below me, there was so much of its
wild parks, mountains and coastline for me still to explore and,
despite all the shame and anguish of being a White South
African, I did not want to be anyone else or live anywhere else.

I got off the plane at Johannesburg's Jan Smuts airport, half-thinking that I would be arrested on the spot. But of course South Africa's hard-pressed security forces had much more threatening opponents to contend with. I was left to board my connecting flight from Johannesburg to Durban, where I moved into my grandmother's flat in Umhlanga Rocks, with its view over the Indian Ocean. She was pleased to have me as a companion because my grandfather had died while I was in London and, very much against her wishes, she had been persuaded to leave Teyateyaneng in order to move closer to my parents.

In order to get my ordeal over with as soon as possible, I immediately wrote to the Exemption Board of the South African Defence Force to tell them that I was back. In case they had mislaid my earlier correspondence, I explained that I was willing to perform a non-military form of national service but that I was not prepared to serve in the military. I asked to be given a definite date for a trial if it was not possible to grant me an alternative. There had been no reply. I suspect that the silence was deliberate and was intended to make me lose my nerve or patience or both, in the hope that I would quietly leave the country, as I had done before, sparing the military the unwelcome publicity of a trial.

The lack of a response faced me with the dilemma of what to do next. After spending a few weeks nervously expecting a knock on the door at any moment, I decided that the best use of my time was to model a non-military form of national service with a view to presenting it at my trial as proof of my readiness to serve an alternative. However, the difficulty of putting the idea into practice was that it required an employer who would be prepared to give me work on the understanding that I was liable at any moment to be 'picked up' by the military police. Given that few organisations would want to risk that or identify themselves with me, finding work was not going to be easy. But, as it turned out, I stumbled upon a project which would have provided an ideal setting for national service and which was to lead me on a personal journey of discovery that would open my eyes to South Africa's colonial past.

Outside the well-watered gardens of Durban's White suburbs, rural Natal was experiencing one of Africa's frequent droughts. No rain had fallen for months; the cattle were dying, and now people too. The crisis was reported in the daily paper, which carried an article about the Valley Trust, a church agricultural project, which claimed to have developed a nutritious new winter-feed. I decided to investigate whether the feed could form part of a wider response to the drought. As I knew next to nothing about the Zulu, in spite of having spent my entire schooling among them in Natal, I took the opportunity to read up the history of the Zulu nation. My main source was the impressively researched book *The Washing of the Spears* by Donald Morris, an American naval officer living in Washington, DC, who, as a young boy of ten, had been fascinated by an account of the Zulu defeat of the British army at Isandhlwana and then, as an adult, had been encouraged by Ernest Hemingway to write a history of the Zulu war of 1879.

From my reading of *The Washing of the Spears*, I learnt that the empire of Shaka, the legendary king of the Zulu, was possibly the largest and most powerful in Africa. At its height in the 1820s, this military genius and ruthless tyrant kept over 50,000 men constantly under arms and laid claim to a vast area that would now take in all of Zululand, Natal and much of northern Transvaal. I could not help speculating how different the history of Southern Africa and my own story would have turned out had this African empire succeeded in repelling the British invasion and had consolidated its power into the twentieth century.

But that was not to be. By the end of the nineteenth century, the territory left to the Zulus in Natal had shrunk to eight impoverished native reserves where, after the Zulu war of 1879, the Zulus not needed to work on White farms had been penned and largely forgotten about. My journey took me to one of these reserves and, while the British were directly responsible for what I was to find, I discovered that Bantu, Boer and Briton all shared some of the blame.

No one knows exactly where the Bantu, the African race of which the Zulu are a part, came from. What is known is that, prior to the arrival of the Europeans, with only scattered groups of the hunter-gatherer San people inhabiting the southern part of the African continent, the Bantu had been able to gradually expand southwards from Central Africa in search of new grazing for their ever-expanding herds of cattle. This migration was essential for them because their civilisation was based exclusively on cattle. A man's wealth and status was decided by how many cattle he owned. He had to purchase a wife with cattle. His diet was mainly meat and milk from his cattle. When the Zulu king wanted to impress foreign guests he did so by running his herds past in a kind of modern military parade. When so much was vested in cattle, their numbers were bound to increase beyond the grazing capacity of a region.

By Shaka's day, the southward expansion of the Bantu was blocked at the Fish River by the northward expansion of the Boers and British from the Cape colony. This had thrown Bantu civilisation into crisis. With no more room to expand, the separate small clans kept bumping into each other; the stronger ones prevailed and amalgamated the smaller and weaker. Warlords, such as Shaka, emerged to consolidate whole tribes and to drive out others. This was the dreadful time known in Bantu folklore as the *Mfecane* or The Crushing, which saw much of the centre of Southern Africa emptied of its African population. Shaka's reign of terror was particularly severe because he insisted on conscripting the entire adult male population and only allowed his warriors to marry after they had 'washed their spears' in battle. His impis were ever on the march, extending the Zulu empire further and further from the royal kraal and forcing the inhabitants of the ravaged hinterland to live as fugitives in the most inaccessible mountainous areas. As a result, great swathes of land appeared to the early

European settlers to be largely uninhabited and therefore ripe for possession. Indeed, the early British and Dutch settlers were reported to have entered a land littered more with skeletons than inhabited by people.

In addition to helping create the conditions for European settlement, Shaka, who had an insatiable curiosity about European civilisation, made the tactical mistake of granting permission for a permanent British trading post to be established at Port Natal, later to be renamed Durban, in 1824. The settlers gradually expanded the colony outwards by extracting further land grants from Shaka and local clan leaders in exchange for European goods and military assistance. Following the usual pattern, these commercial and agricultural ventures formed a spearhead for empire: once the settlement had reached a sufficient size, it warranted protection and so troops were sent; the settlement needed to be organised, so colonial administrators were sent; the warlike ways of the natives posed a threat and so missionaries were sent. So the colony grew but, in ever constant danger from the unpredictable Zulu king to the north, who had no concept of handing over permanent title to his land, the still small number of settlers dared not expand their holdings much beyond the area around Port Natal, where they could hastily retreat and, if one was in port, find sanctuary on board a ship.

In 1839, the number of Europeans in Natal was swollen overnight by an influx of Boers. They were part of the Great Trek, a mass exodus of the mainly Dutch inhabitants of the Cape Colony, which had been annexed by Britain from Holland during the Napoleonic wars. After creating independent republics in the Orange Free State and Transvaal, a group crossed the Drakensberg Mountains, separating the hinterland from the coastal strip, with the intention of creating a third Boer republic in Natal. At a time when the Zulu nation was reeling from the final years of Shaka's tyranny, when, after the death of his mother, he turned on his own people, alienated the army and was assassinated by his half-brother Dingane, their coming started to tip the balance of power in Natal away from the Zulu.

Shaka's successor, the cunning Dingane, correctly sized up the Boer threat. He peacefully received the delegation sent to negotiate territory. Then he disarmingly signed a paper ceding them the whole of Natal before luring them into the royal kraal for a farewell dance. Once there, with the shout, *'Bambani abaThaKathi!'* (Kill the wizards), he had them seized and taken to be impaled on stakes at the place of execution on a hill outside the kraal, and in full view of the home of horrified American missionaries. He then sent several of his regiments against the unsuspecting Boers camped in the foothills of the Drakensberg. The resulting massacres imprinted on the Afrikaner mind what ever since has been called the *swart gevaar* (black threat). The survivors reported finding a pregnant woman with her belly cut open and her foetus dashed against a wagon, a woman with her breasts cut off and a castrated man with his testicles shoved into his mouth. With such graphic reports and a large number of men, women and children killed, it is understandable that the fledgeling Boer nation should forge a steely resolve never to compromise its security in a country where it would always be a small minority.

Fortunately for the European settlers, the balance of power then swung further away from the Zulus, when a large clan under another of the royal brothers, Mpande, defected from Zululand and allied with the Boers against Dingane. This enabled the Boers to exact their revenge on Dingane at the battle of Blood River and to install Mpande as a pliant king in Zululand. Emboldened by these military successes, they then sought to extend their republic of New Holland to the whole of Natal by bringing the British settlement at Port Natal under their control. The resulting siege of the small British garrison posed a challenge to the British in the Cape, who, up till then, had refused to countenance the expense of annexing Natal and the military risk of having to defend it against the warlike Zulu. A contingent of troops was sent on board ship up the coast to lift the siege. After defeating the Boers, without consulting the Zulu, whose territory it was, the British commander then annexed Natal as a district of the Cape Colony. This restricted the Zulu from 1845 to an independent kingdom north of the Tugela River.

With a colonial administration in place in Natal, there was now a rush by Briton and Boer to make formal land claims. The two largest claims recorded give some idea of the scale of the dispossession of those Bantu who had formerly relied on the land now being parcelled out to European settlers. A certain Commandant Rudolf laid claim to forty farms totalling 400,000 acres. A Mr Aspeling, who resided in Cape Town, invoked Shaka's initial grant, which he held to have come his way by marriage, to claim 3,500 square miles. While all the outrageous claims were rejected, the newly appointed British High Commissioner for Natal recognised land claims totalling millions of acres of the best farmland.

The permanent dispossession of the original African population of Natal was completed when the new colonial administration created special native reserves to deal with the massive influx of refugee tribes, who took the opportunity of the *pax Britannica* in Natal to return to where their ancestors had lived before Shaka's terror. Initially many settled as squatters on farms now owned by Europeans. By the 1850s, it was estimated that there were about 150,000 of them and that their number grew to over 250,000 as more of the refugees returned from further afield. Rather than accommodate them by reducing the size of the newly created White farms and granting them title to the land freed up, such was the perceived threat posed by the imbalance between Black and White, that the bulk of the African population was shifted by a combination of force and inducements into eight major reserves, strategically chosen not to interfere with the new European settlements and placed to act as buffers against the tribes living across the Natal border. The Secretary for Native Affairs, Theophilus Shepstone, justified the policy on the grounds that it would help preserve the native's African culture and traditions. However, the land allocated for the reserves was woefully inadequate and amounted to barely more than a million acres.

After the dispersal of the African population to the native reserves, the last major threat to the new colony remained the militaristic kingdom of Zululand on its northern border. The ineffectual Mpande, who had been content to grow enormously fat and to spend all his time in his seraglio, had been succeeded by his son, Cetswayho, a proud, athletic figure, who was not content to rule as a mere puppet of the British. Nevertheless, Cetswayho was sufficient of a statesman not to provoke hostilities and kept his impis north of the Tugela River and within what had become his western border with the Boers in the Transvaal. But then friction arose over territory the Boer settlers encroached upon and which the Zulus had tradition-ally regarded as their grazing lands. Despite an independent commission upholding the Zulu claims, the colonial office suppressed the report in the interests of realpolitik. This recognised that for there to be a lasting peace in Natal, the power of the Zulu, under their militaristic kings with their standing army of at least 20,000 warriors, had to be broken once and for all. A decision was taken to launch a pre-emptive strike.

Queen Victoria's darling general Lord Chelmsford led the campaign in 1879. He completely underestimated his opponents and arrogantly ignored the advice of the local settlers, which allowed the Zulus to display their military prowess before the war achieved its predictable outcome. At Isandhlwana Zulu impis cut off and wiped out half of Chelmsford's unprepared forces, killing some 900 troops with about the same number of African levies. Such was the debacle that, in the interests of salvaging Britain's injured pride, as much as possible was made of the desperate defence later that day of Rorke's Drift, where a handful of British soldiers repulsed an attack by massed ranks of Zulu warriors and were awarded eleven Victoria Crosses. Fortunately for the British, the assegai was no match for the Model 1871 Martini-Henry single-shot breech-loading rifle, especially when shot as battalion volley fire from a range of 600 to 800 yards. When the Zulu army made one final, heroic attempt to defend their king before the royal kraal of Ulundi, they were slaughtered in their thousands, with none able to get within thirty yards of the famous British square. Cetswayho was captured, exiled to Robben Island and Zululand was formally annexed as part of Natal.

While for all practical purposes, the history of the Zulu empire was ended by the war, it is worth recalling the protests of the one dissenting voice among the British in Natal, that of its first bishop, John William Colenso. In England, Bishop Colenso had been branded a heretic for having questioned the verbal inspiration of Scripture by showing, with the aid of mathematics, that the story of the Exodus could not possibly be literally true. At a time when imperial Britain was at the height of her power and prone to see the religions of her imperial subjects as inferior to Christianity, he also took a more inclusive approach to non-Christian religions. These pioneering thoughts did not sit comfortably with the religious certainties of the day.

In Natal he was an equally controversial figure and deeply unpopular with the colonists. After taking the trouble to learn the Zulu language, which enabled him to listen and understand the grievances of the natives from their perspective, he had taken to championing their side when they were unjustly treated. He had also publicly fallen out with Sir Theophilus Shepstone by defending a chief, Langalibalele, who had committed the great offence of defying Shepstone's total power over the so-called Natal kaffirs. The hapless chief had been tried in the Natal courts in a way that Colenso held to be contrary to the tradition of British justice. After he had been found guilty, the colonists had virtually forced his tribe into slavery.

When the Zulu war ended, Colenso returned to England to plead for the return of Cetswayho on the grounds that the Zulus had only ever fought a defensive war. He succeeded in winning approval for the king to be shipped from Robben Island to put his case personally before Queen Victoria. Once in London, the commanding figure of the warrior king, who had defeated the mighty British army at Isandhlwana, swayed public feeling towards the Zulu. The government relented and allowed his return to Zululand. But no sooner had he returned than the Natal colonial administration, smarting from Colenso's triumph, thwarted the restoration of a Zulu kingdom by imposing terms which drastically reduced its size and by supporting a rival chief in the north of Zululand, who had made off with much of the king's cattle and some of his wives after the battle of Ulundi. Before long, Zululand was in a state of civil war. The northern chief defeated Cetswayho's forces and the king was hunted down and killed. The turmoil inside Zululand then provided the pretext for the Natal colonial administration to take complete control of the territory. Such was the disappointment to him of this final chapter of the Zulu kingdom, that Bishop Colenso died a broken and defeated man.

With the only effective Black opposition to White supremacy in Southern Africa destroyed, life in the over-populated Natal native reserves would continue relatively peacefully over the next hundred years. With a limit to the number of cattle the reserves were capable of providing grazing for, the residents would increasingly come to depend on migrant labour in the mines, farms and cities of White South Africa. It is difficult to judge whether general conditions were any worse in 1980 than they were in 1880. Suffice to say that when drought struck there was nowhere to move the cattle and so they died in their thousands. The people who were dependent on them then simply died of starvation. Such was the still air of resignation about these reserves, that anyone entering them could not but be struck by the way all the inhabitants seemed to move slowly, as if they were grimly concentrating on survival. One only needed to look closely enough at the distended bellies of the malnourished children, the vacant eyes of the young men doped on dagga (marijuana), who in Shaka's day would have been fearsome warriors, and the emaciated dignity of the old to see the signs of quiet desperation everywhere.

The Valley Trust, my destination in my quest for a model of non-military national service, was founded as a response to this deprivation. It was based at Msinga in the remote Tugela valley of northern Natal. The link with the Anglican Church was at best tenuous and probably amounted to little more than the provision of some funding, as it was not a Christian mission, at least not in any recognisable sense. There were no church buildings, school, hospital and houses for the expatriate clergy, doctors and teachers, usually associated with a traditional African mission station. Instead, when I approached where the project was supposed to be on my map, all there was to see were dense thickets of acacia trees lining the banks of the Tugela River. I had to leave my car by the side of the road and to walk into the trees before finding, perched above the river like an eyrie, the home of Neil and Creena Alcock.

This remarkable couple were pioneers of an altogether different kind of Christian mission. They started from the principle that the missionary should only possess those things also available to the indigenous population. Their aim was to model how the local people could raise their standard of living by using local resources combined with simple innovative technology. Neil, for instance, constructed a methane digester out of a pair of drums, which used the gas given off by rotting vegetation and cow dung to provide a source of renewable energy for their home cooking. Creena, by creating an irrigation system on the bank of the river, had developed a market garden to supplement the mainly meat and milk diet of the Zulu. As the paper I had read reported, they had improved the quality of livestock in the area by developing a highly nutritious winter-feed for cattle and goats by gathering and mulching the thorns of the ubiquitous acacia tree.

When Neil and Creena heard about my predicament over military service, they welcomed me as a kindred spirit and put me up in an isolated wattle and daub hut kept for volunteers about half a mile downriver from their home. True to their principles, the hut contained nothing that was European, such as a bed. Its only item of furniture was a simple reed mat. After they left me, I made myself a fire and settled down to cook myself a meal. Then there was little else to do but sit and watch the water, the birds and one of Africa's sunsets, which grow and grow and grow until, seemingly bursting with praise for the creator, the sun fills the heavens with fretted fire.

I woke stiff and cold in the morning. After breakfast, I sat with a mug of coffee in the sunshine looking out at the river and listened to the birdsong. When I had thawed out and my muscles had recovered from the unforgiving mud floor, I decided that, with a full belly, there could be no more enchanting place. The peace and solitude were deeply soothing until a group of women came to fill their water jars and to wash clothes and bathe on the opposite bank. I should have slipped away. But the beauty of their forms rooted me to the spot. Watching them, I understood why John Dunn, the early renegade English settler favoured by Cetswayho and used as his interpreter in negotiations with the other settlers, came to have as many as forty-nine Zulu wives. His descendants are now a Zulu tribe in their own right. I mused on the thought that the future of South Africa might have turned out entirely differently if more of the early settlers had 'gone native' and followed Dunn's example.

The main problem I encountered in this disturbing wilderness was security. Unlike Neil and Creena, I had brought with me all the camping equipment a European would expect to carry for such an expedition, such as a sleeping bag, rucksack and ample provisions. I had also driven down in my grandmother's new car, which I had parked some distance from my hut because the last part of the track was inaccessible. I had worried about it all night and so, when I was eventually able to drag myself away from watching naked ladies, I set off to reassure myself that it was still there. I had not gone more than a few hundred metres when a group of small boys passed me. We greeted each other cheerily enough and then a sixth sense warned me that they seemed to be walking rather purposefully in the direction of my hut, which was not locked and in which were all my worldly possessions. I thereupon turned and raced back, to discover them all inside. One managed to escape through the window with tins of food. The others I cornered in the hut, and not knowing what else to do, I seized the largest boy by the arm and took him, followed by the others, to Neil Alcock. He wagged a gentle finger at them and let them go. He then explained that, without a police force in the area, the only real security was to possess nothing worth stealing. In so many words, he challenged me to live in the real Africa.

I think I would have gladly accepted this challenge if I could have stayed on indefinitely at Msinga. But, as attractive as the thought of setting myself up as a John Dunn was, I had no means of sustaining myself. Therefore, after spending a few days more with two of the most radical people I have ever met and having eaten up all my provisions, I reluctantly returned to Durban.

On my return, I was so enthralled by all that I had seen Neil and Creena doing that I wrote a proposal for a non-military form of national service to be performed in rural development projects. Essentially what I proposed was a kind of British VSO or United States Peace Corps for South Africa. I accepted that conscientious objectors would need to be screened by a tribunal and, to compensate for the hardship and danger of military service, should serve for a longer period. I ended by justifying the provision of an alternative to the waste of thousands of young people emigrating to evade military service, the pointlessness of imprisoning people whose skills might constructively be used in the service of their country, and the fact that deteriorating conditions in South Africa's drought-stricken rural areas posed an equal if not greater threat to the country's long-term security than the threat it faced on its borders.

Hoping that he might be my champion, I travelled all the way to Pretoria to deliver my proposed non-military form of national service in person to the Chaplain General of the South African Defence Force. He received it politely enough, but, along with similar proposals from other concerned individuals, such was the military's fear of opening the floodgates to conscientious objection, that it was consigned to the dustbin. I still think it the best idea I have ever had for improving the world and regard its rejection as an important moment in my growing up.

My visit to Msinga did have one positive outcome though. Alison had mentioned while we were in London that she was required to do a medical elective, which could be in a developing country, as part of her medical training. After my broadening experience of rural Africa, I wondered whether she would gain from a similar experience and could not help thinking how lovely it would be to share this land and its people with her. But even as I fondly pictured us living and working together in one of the rural mission stations, I worried that the colonial Africa of which that dream was a part had gone for ever. I also understood that the legacy of apartheid would be to leave the new South Africa marked by endemic violence because it looked as if the prophecy of the Zulu priest Stephen Kumalo, in *Cry the Beloved Country*, had come to pass: 'I fear that when the White man turns to loving, we shall have turned to hating.'

I therefore saw no future in our relationship and once again resolved not to encourage it beyond friendship. Nevertheless, I wrote to Alison and offered to explore an elective for her at the Bethesda Mission Hospital in northern Zululand, where I knew the medical director could be relied upon to ensure that she would have a worthwhile experience of rural African medicine and be safe. With the letter, I sent her a copy of *The Washing of the Spears*.

3

JUNE 16

You cannot love an abstraction: neither can you trust it: you can only know and love a person. It is the aim of the Government of South Africa to make it impossible for a White South African to know and love a Black South African.

(Trevor Huddleston, *Naught For Your Comfort*)

The possibility of Alison serving her medical elective in South Africa pleased but also unnerved me. She had not ventured south of the equator before and I expected conditions in rural Africa would come as something of a shock. What if the raw medicine she was bound to encounter proved too much for her? Brought up in comfortable Surrey and the daughter of an eminent scientist, she was also bound to come out with many of the political ideals and prejudices of the educated English middle and upper classes. Who would she blame for apartheid? Would she be dismayed by our lack of culture? And, if I was still at large and she visited me in Durban, what would she make of my family, and, in particular, of my mother – an Afrikaner? And what would my mother make of her?

My anxiety needs to be understood against the background of a country divided, not only between Black and White, but also between English and Afrikaner. Moreover, the level of dislike and mistrust between the two European nations in

South Africa was, if anything, greater than that between the Afrikaner and the Bantu, who had a kind of grudging respect for each other; with the patronising, liberal English, one never really knew where one stood. In the eyes of the Afrikaner, the English had also stolen the country and practised apartheid in Africa long before anyone else. I was keenly aware of this long history from my mother's side of the family, who were descended from one of the earliest Cape settler families, the van Reenens.

According to the research of my cousin John George, a keen genealogist, Jacob von Rhenen was born in 1703 in the Baltic port of Memel, Lithuania. The story goes that he fled to the Cape after fighting a duel and killing his opponent. He became a burgher (a free citizen) and prospered, supplying meat to the Dutch East India Company from at least seven farms. The official records show that he owned numerous slaves and over twenty-six freehold properties in Cape Town. His grave, that of his wife, Johanna, who was born in Amsterdam, and members of their family can be seen in Cape Town on what was then the family farm, Welgelegen, of which all that remains is one of the city's oldest buildings, Mostert's Mill.

By the time the British formally annexed the Cape in 1812, Jacob's sons, Johannes Gysbertus, Jacob and Sebastian Valentyn, had helped to establish the basis of the South African wool industry. They were also among the leading wine growers and were the first to introduce Arab horses and London drays to the Cape. If history was not so capricious, the descendants of Jacob von Rhenen or van Reenen, as his sons signed themselves, would today be farming hugely valuable Cape wine farms and owning much of the freehold of Cape Town itself. Instead, the family joined the Great Trek, the mass exodus of settlers from British rule into the interior of Southern Africa, which started in earnest after 1834, when the slave economy of the Cape was thrown into crisis with the abolition of slavery throughout the British Empire.

Like the biblical story of the exodus of the Jews from Egypt, the story of the Great Trek has taken on mythical proportions in Afrikaner folklore. A visit to the imposing Voortrekker Monument outside Pretoria leaves the impression of one continuous long line of wagons snaking into the wilderness, whereas the reality was of a more gradual migration over decades, with the trekkers leaving family behind to keep open their lines of supply in the Cape. There were still van Reenens in the Cape in 1863, for instance, because my great grandfather Johannes Hendrik van Reenen is recorded as having been born in Cape Town in that year. Nevertheless, many of the original Cape settler families left for good to start all over again in the untamed and menacing interior.

The trekkers' main grievance was that English missionaries insisted that the law abolishing slavery be upheld on their vast farms, many of them miles from Cape Town and, more importantly, miles from an alternative supply of labour. The new law therefore posed a serious threat to their 'lekker lewe' (good life) in the sunny and mild Mediterranean climate of the Cape. Colonial administrators intent on Anglicising the mainly Dutch culture were also irritants. But it must have been the news that the interior was largely uninhabited and good farming country, which explains why so many got up and left so much behind. And spectacular country it certainly was. Once over Namaqualand, with its gorgeous spring flower show, and the sun-scorched plains of the Karoo, the country opened up into wide grasslands beyond the Orange River. The area to the west of the Caledon River, just over the border from what became Basutoland, was especially attractive and fertile and it was there, in the closer of the two new Boer Republics, the Oranje Vry Staat, that Johannes Hendrik van Reenen chose to settle on the farm Barletta.

I can dimly remember Barletta. The farmhouse was built out of local stone, quarried from the mountain at the back. It had a corrugated iron roof, painted green, and a long cool veranda, running the length of the house. I can just recall the view from the veranda of formal rose gardens, a clay tennis court and fields of maize and sunflower, which stretched as far as the eye could see. In less than a hundred years, the van Reenens, with the help of their farm workers, had transformed a wilderness and had helped establish the valuable cereal farming of the eastern Orange Free State.

But no matter how far the Boers trekked away from the Cape, the British came after them – not that they were after the troublesome fugitives themselves. First, diamonds were discovered in 1867 in Griqualand West, which was disputably part of the Orange Free State. Soon what is now the Great Hole at Kimberley started to emerge as swarms of prospectors from all over the world arrived to dig. The British were quick to act and annexed the diamond fields in 1871, which the Boers were apparently willing to consent to in return for a one-off payment of a paltry £90,000. But then the fate of the two Boer republics was sealed when gold was discovered on the Rand in the Transvaal in 1886. Despite Britain having officially recognised the two Boer republics in 1851, it was now a foregone conclusion that the Boers, who wanted simply to be left to their farming, would once again be put under the irksome thumb of the English.

Initially the British hoped that, with a show of force, war might be avoided. On the first attempt in 1877, troops marched from Natal into the Transvaal, hoisted the Union Jack in front of a crowd of bemused Boers in their capital, Pretoria, and declared the two Boer republics annexed to the Crown. After some hesitation, the Boers saw them off. They were as fearless as the Zulu but were expert marksmen. Family legend has it that my great-grandfather prided himself on having been brought up to stalk and kill an antelope at a thousand metres with a rifle; how much easier a target was the British soldier in his red tunic. And, very frustrating for the 'red necks', the Boers would not stand and fight. After a humiliating defeat at Majuba, the first British expeditionary force was obliged to retreat to the safety of Natal to await the arrival of more troops.

In 1899 the army was ready and invaded the Transvaal for

a second time. The Boers put up a dogged resistance and their guerrilla tactics might have succeeded were it not for all that was at stake under the ground. They were finally over-whelmed in 1902 by force of numbers and a scorched earth policy, which put many of their farms, including Barletta, with much of its exquisite stinkwood furniture, to the torch. The British general Lord Kitchener also ruthlessly ordered Boer women and children, including my great-grandmother and her children, into the first concentration camps. Despite the protests of English women, such as Emily Hobhouse, many died of disease in the camps, leaving a lasting bitterness.

My mother, who lived at Barletta until she married, was told many stories of the concentration camps. They formed, along with stories of the Great Trek, the Day of the Covenant, which the Boers swore before the battle of Blood River, Spion Kop and other heroic Boer war victories, a body of Afrikaner folklore that defined them and set them apart from the English. She recalls a blissfully happy upbringing on the farm. Her favourite memory is of her father, Johannes Rynholdt van Reenen, whistling as he rode back from the fields in the morning. The tune would warn of his arrival and, with her mother and sister, she would scramble to join him for breakfast, fully dressed and fully made up. They were after all Dutch ladies of fine breeding and my grandfather never let them forget it. One can understand why my father, Norman Yeats, one of the hillbilly English traders from across the Basutoland border, known for their polo and wild partying, was not exactly welcome as a suitor.

After the Boer surrender, Britain was finally able to com-plete the unification of its two colonies, the Cape and Natal (which now included Zululand), with the two former Boer republics of the Orange Free State and Transvaal in the Union of South Africa of 1910. It was a triumph for Cecil John Rhodes, the imperialist and financial genius, who, with the backing of the largest bank in the world, the Rothschild Bank, was left a free hand to develop the South African mining industry. For the benefit of a small Western elite, his Anglo-American Corporation and De Beers, with the help of laws passed by the new South African government, proceeded to harness the people of an entire subcontinent to dig for diamonds and gold under conditions of virtual slavery. Recruiting centres for the mines were set up throughout Southern Africa to take on men and send them to the Great Hole at Kimberley or to Igoli, the City of Gold. Their journey is movingly described in the lament by the internationally renowned South African trumpeter, Hugh Masekela, 'The Train to Johannesburg', which vividly describes the miner's sense of loss at leaving behind loved ones for the single-sex mine hostels, infested with cockroaches and violent crime, and the steaming earth, miles underground.

Having secured her commercial interests, Britain was content to hand executive power in South Africa back to a government made up of English and Afrikaner politicians, headed by Boers. The first Prime Minister was Louis Botha, a former Boer general. The second Prime Minister, Jan Smuts, also a former Boer general, was to emerge as an international statesmen after the First World War and lived on to dominate South African politics until the end of the Second World War as leader of the United Party. This coalition of former enemies succeeded in uniting English and Afrikaner against a diehard minority of Afrikaner nationalists, who wanted nothing to do with the hated English and went so far as to stage an unsuccessful military rebellion in opposition to South Africa's entry into the First World War on the side of the Allies.

My grandfather was a staunch supporter of the United Party. In many ways he exemplified all that was best in the progressive Afrikaner community and, while, like Jan Smuts, he was certainly not a strict democrat, he treated his Black farmworkers fairly and cared for their families. He held, with some reason, that Westminster-style democracy was a recipe for national disaster in a situation where Whites were out-numbered four to one by Blacks, who were mostly still illiterate and had no experience of democracy. Instead, like many of the more enlightened Afrikaners, he believed in a limited democracy, with the gradual extension of the franchise to include educated and propertied Blacks. When these political convictions were challenged by liberal critics, such as Helen Suzman, who deserted the United Party to form the Progressive Party in 1959, he argued that the slow pace of democratic reform explained the stability of Britain's democracy. He would also point out that it was not that long ago when the Irish, who emigrated to South Africa and fought in the Irish Brigade against the British in the Boer War, were subject to repressive laws, which excluded Catholics from the vote, from owning land, from carrying a sword and even from educating their children.

The tragedy, however, for enlightened Afrikaners like my grandfather, is that the paternalistic politics of the United Party were not sustainable in a country where Whites were a small minority and where the British had bequeathed them a flawed democratic constitution. By the standards of the day, this constitution, which denied the black majority the vote, and provided no mechanism for the progressive extension of the franchise, was probably all that could be hoped for. But, without pressure from Britain for the gradual inclusion of Black voters, someone was bound sooner or later to play the race card. And, with Britain preoccupied with German militarism from the date the constitution was signed in 1910 until apartheid proper became official policy in 1948, there is a certain inevitability about what happened.

Nevertheless, British colonial policy might have done more to avert tragedy. It consistently failed the Black opposition, who reacted to the Act of Union by forming the African National Native Congress in 1912, later renamed the African National Congress (ANC), and dedicated their movement to extending the franchise to all on a non-racial basis. Successive Black delegations were sent to London to plead with the king for fair play and justice, but only to be disappointed. The frustration they felt drove some to turn to more radical politics and, in 1921, the South African Communist Party (SACP) was formed to fight for an 'independent native republic' as a precursor to a socialist state. This response, again understandable at the time, was, from hindsight, a grave mistake because, while the objective of a two-stage revolution did not persuade many in the Black community, the close links between the SACP and ANC undermined support for the ANC in Britain and in the United States. In South Africa the *rooi gevaar* (red threat) could now be combined with the *swart gevaar* to really scare the voters.

The critical moment for the Crown, still constitutionally the supreme power in South Africa, was the election of 1948. In this year, the White supremacists of the Nationalist Party, playing on the electorate's fears, defeated Smuts's United Party, and set about entrenching racism at every level of society. The cornerstone of new government legislation was the Group Areas Act, which enforced segregation in each city, town and village by requiring each racial group to live in its own area. While the resulting racially stratified societ' improved security for the minority White population, it left Africans always fourth in the pecking order, after the Asian and so-called Coloured or mixed-race communities, and forced them to travel great distances to work or to the shops. The physical separation also made it virtually impossible for members of the different races to meet together as persons.

The notion of racial purity was promoted at every turn. Despite the existence of a large mixed-race group, the Immorality Act was passed to prohibit sexual relations between the races. This draconian law was enforced by means of identification cards, with the race of each person imprinted on the card. It was especially cruel for so-called Coloureds who could pass themselves off as White and who had married Whites; they were now exposed before lovers, family and friends as non-White. It also involved invasive surveillance of private homes and intimate physical examinations of Black women suspected of having had intercourse with White men.

For any White man or young boy caught in such a *liaison dangereuse*, such was the shame that many committed suicide rather than face a public trial. Rigid censorship of films, newspapers, magazines and books reinforced the nation's fear of sexual impurity of any kind.

With only muted protests from the Crown, the Nationalist government's racist programme went unchallenged and culminated in the homeland policy of Hendrik Verwoed, the architect of grand apartheid. He became Prime Minister in 1958 and took over and developed Theophilus Shepstone's policy of separate reserves for the Natal 'kaffirs' by creating self-governing Bantustans for each of South Africa's main Black ethnic groups. These homelands were supposed, with White South Africa's help, to evolve into viable independent states. But as so often happens with social engineering on a vast scale, Verwoed's impossible vision ran ahead of the available resources. Instead of creating model states, the homelands became ghettos for the disposal of surplus population. They were also a convenient means of denying the majority Black population a vote in South Africa because, by becoming citizens of a homeland, they lost their South African citizenship.

My grandfather was genuinely appalled and did his best to have the United Party re-elected in his local constituency of Ladybrand. I know something about the efforts he made because, with no school thought suitable for White children in Basutoland, after my mother taught me at home for a year, I was sent to live with my Afrikaner grandparents in order to attend their local Afrikaans school in Ladybrand. I well remember the evening they entertained the then leader of the United Party and Official Opposition Sir De Villiers Graaf, or 'Div' as they affectionately called him. His visit was heralded, much to my excitement, by a group of security policemen, who positioned themselves at the four corners of the garden. It felt as if the house was under siege, which, in a sense it was, but not by Blacks, but by fellow Afrikaners who had rejected the United Party for the naked racism of the Nationalist Party.

Fortunately, Oupa did not live through the next stage of the unfolding tragedy, because he would have been devastated by the increasingly violent turn it took. The ANC initially reacted to the Nationalist Party victory by launching a non-violent defiance campaign against apartheid, and more specifically against the pass laws, which were introduced to enforce the Group Areas Act. This tested the limits of civil disobedience and the commitment to non-violence of the ANC leadership under its devout Christian President, Chief Albert Luthuli. But after protests led to the Sharpeville massacre of 1961, in which the police turned their guns on a crowd of unarmed civilians, and to the imposition of a state of emergency in which the ANC, Communist Party and the newly formed Pan-Africanist Congress (PAC) were banned, Black political parties were forced underground and into exile. The ban decided ANC leaders such as Nelson Mandela that politics had to be carried on by other means and he helped form and lead its military wing *Umkhonto we Sizwe* until his arrest in 1962. From the launch of Umkhonto, South Africa descended into a state of civil war.

For all the high drama of these years, my generation and that of my parents were mostly unaware that the country was at war with itself. The South African military was easily able to contain the low intensity guerrilla war of the 1960s and early 1970s because the few military bases the ANC were able to set up in Angola and Zambia were too far away to pose a real military threat. I was also shielded by my all-White boarding school in Natal, which provided a secure haven from the gathering political storm outside. But by the mid 1970s, this abruptly changed when the exiled ANC managed to bring the guerrilla war closer to White South Africa by persuading Black youth to reject Bantu education and to make the townships ungovernable. As I have recounted, the strategy succeeded spectacularly in my second year as a university student with the Soweto uprising of 16 June 1976. The aftershocks rapidly spread to other urban areas and soon every township was, if not literally then metaphorically ablaze, in open revolt against the apartheid regime. And this time, there was no going back because the schoolchildren had decisively turned their back on the future apartheid intended for them.

In the light of this history, which I intended to tell Alison about when she visited, I hoped that she would not be too hard on the Afrikaner and, in particular, my mother. In advance of the visit, I even pondered whether to send her my prized copy of Alan Paton's biography of Jan Hofmeyer, the brilliant protégé of Smuts: a Rhodes Scholar at sixteen, Professor of Classics at twenty-two, Administrator of the Transvaal at twenty-nine and then Minister of Finance in the war cabinet. Alan Paton clearly saw Hofmeyer as a future Afrikaner leader who had the courage, intellect and faith to save South Africa. But, like so many human tragedies, apartheid was beyond the powers of any one individual to control, and once set in train, it became virtually impossible to change direction, until all sides had plumbed the depths of human suffering and had come to recognise that there had to be a better way.

In this light, the terrible violence of the township youth has to be seen as crucial for the emergence of the new South Africa, because they forced a time of reckoning, not only for Whites but also for Blacks. Any Black person suspected of collaborating with the hated regime became liable to be executed by 'necklacing', a form of execution that involved a tyre doused in petrol being placed around the victim and set alight. Unavoidably, there were other excesses. The climate of fear and suspicion encouraged witch-hunts and thuggery. Ordinary, law-abiding people became brutalised and participated in the killings. The horrific violence forced the White electorate to recognise that if the military and police patrols lost the battle for the townships, as there was every possibility they could, the killing would spill out of the townships and into the White areas. White women talked of gang rape and grew hysterical. Those Whites who could follow the flight of capital tended, as I had done, to leave the country.

But many Whites who could have left chose not to. In Durban, under the inspired leadership of Archbishop Hurley, the previously conservative churches responded to the watershed of 16 June by founding Diakonia as a focus of their opposition to apartheid and in an attempt to keep open lines of communication between the White and Black communities. The project was initially based in ramshackle offices in downtown Durban, but later moved into the buildings of a disused convent, which was renovated and modernised to provide office accommodation for a diverse number of anti-apartheid organisations. The first director was a Catholic layperson, Paddy Kearney, a slight, bearded figure, with a shy and disarming smile, who helped Diakonia become such a thorn in the side of the apartheid regime that, at the height of the unrest, the once peaceful convent was completely surrounded by police and army vehicles to prevent anyone getting away while searches were made of all the offices.

When, shortly after my return from the Valley Trust and after I had submitted my model of non-military national service to the Chaplain General of the SADF, Paddy asked me to join Diakonia, I jumped at the opportunity. With its multiracial staff and involvement in the Black community, it presented me with a rare opportunity to share in the emergence of the new South Africa. As Archbishop Hurley kept reminding us in those early days, when it was easy to be discouraged by the impossibility of the challenge, it was enough that we should be a community trying to subvert the old system peacefully and to be a sign of the new. His vision was that the project should help develop the civil society that would eventually provide the leadership and governance of a post-apartheid Durban. For those with eyes to see, this emerging leadership could just be seen in the confident, talented and exuberant multiracial community that gathered from time to time at Diakonia. Indeed, one only had to meet respected Black leaders, such as the indomitable Mary Mkhwanazi, the full-time organiser of the South African

Domestic Workers Union, to know that there was no stopping it.

Archbishop Hurley worked tirelessly to unite all the churches in Durban behind Diakonia. His commitment was impressive because the ecumenical movement was a Protestant initiative, to which the Catholic Church has never given its full blessing. I was able to observe his personal commitment at several Diakonia council meetings, where he was fully one of the assembled church leaders. As a result of his efforts, the churches in Durban did have some success in moderating the violence. My hero worship grew and, rejecting the divisions between the churches as religious apartheid, I started to attend the services of all churches and to receive communion wherever I was not barred from the communion rail.

In addition to providing me with experience of a project working to overcome divisions between the races and among the churches, Diakonia also helped make me aware of that other unacceptable divide in the human race: the one between the sexes. Even here, Archbishop Hurley was in the vanguard of his church. To my knowledge he was the first Catholic bishop to publicly acknowledge that there is no good theological reason why a woman should not be ordained a priest. When asked he held that apartheid had opened his eyes on this issue. It was a radical stance for which he paid the price of a cardinal's hat because, despite being the longest-serving Catholic bishop in the world and South Africa's foremost Catholic leader, the conservative Pope John Paul II, who appointed more cardinals than any other pope, would not entrust him with the honour.

Paddy Kearney's partner, Carmel, made a helpful contribution to my own understanding in this area. They were not married at the time and my grandmother thought their relationship highly improper. But what she was unaware of and would not, in any case, have appreciated is that Paddy and Carmel were working at establishing a basis for an equal marriage. This was a revolutionary idea in the context of chauvinist South African society, where White males would not expect to perform even the smallest domestic task and would not have any idea of what equality between the sexes meant. I was no exception and found liberated women baffling and an impossible challenge.

Carmel also brought to my attention the role of women in the anti-apartheid struggle. I learned from her about the March of the Women, which was part of the 1956 Defiance Campaign protesting against the pass laws. This saw over twenty thousand women converge on the Union Buildings in Pretoria chanting as one of their slogans, 'Strike the women and you have struck a rock'. What struck me about Carmel and other leading women dissidents, was that they combined physical powerlessness with a total fearlessness. It was a combination which proved surprisingly effective in confrontations with the security forces because, if it did not exactly disarm heavily armed policemen itching to have a go at protesters, who they were indoctrinated to see at best as irritants and at worst as scum, it at least made the police hesitate to use the full force at their disposal. Astute men quickly learned the lesson that it paid to walk alongside a woman in a protest march.

What with Diakonia exposing me as a male chauvinist, I had probably taken in about as much as I could digest from all my kaleidoscopic experiences since returning to South Africa ten months before. Alison's call late one night from London therefore came as a thankful diversion from the rigours of the liberation struggle. She announced that she had failed Pathology and needed to re-sit the examination the following summer. This meant that she had forfeited her next summer holiday, when she had planned to visit me before starting her elective at Bethesda, and so could she come to stay in ten days' time for the two weeks of her Christmas holiday.

4

ENGLISH ROSE

It is a brilliant morning in Umtata, Transkei, where we are staying in
the Moll's house. Far too light to sleep and so I shall attempt to
gather my thoughts and write a journal of events.

(An English Lady's South African Diary)

On first catching sight of Alison as she emerged from the
airport arrivals gate in a colourful cotton dress, I needed to
draw in breath. Having only seen her swathed in heavy winter
woollens in the few months we had known each other in
London, I had not realised how unlike the slim and tanned
South African girls she was. She had the figure of a young
woman with a healthy appetite. In the bright sunshine, she
looked strikingly pale. Coming from the fog and ice of London,
she was unprepared for the sweltering heat of an African
summer and was so hot that she was glowing all over. To
crown it all, there was the Titian hair.

    She later confided that my appearance had also come as
something of a surprise to her. I was no longer the clean-
shaven young man in a suit she had known in London for I
wore shorts and sandals and had grown a beard. The last was
in anticipation of going to detention barracks where the rules
permitted a prisoner to keep his beard and where there would
be little point in shaving. I had been so absorbed that I had not

thought of warning her and she initially failed to recognise me in the throng. This gave me a moment to get my breath back, to observe this altogether foreign creature, and then to sense, as I always do on first seeing her, the laughter bubbling up inside me.

Feeling lighter than I had for months, I drove Alison home to meet my grandmother, who I knew would break Alison into the family in a gentle way. She was thrilled that I had brought home a girl from England, and the two women speedily entered into an alliance. My grandmother's belief in all things English was not the only factor though. She was a shrewd judge of character and immediately sized Alison up as a woman with whom she could do business.

After tea, I was sent off on an errand while the two women settled down to a private conversation. My grandmother lost no time in telling Alison that she needed to see that I shaved my beard as it really did not suit me and, in any case, Yeats men did not wear beards. She also made it clear that she disapproved of Diakonia and especially of Paddy Kearney. She insisted that Alison make me understand that there was no future in the kind of work I was doing and that the sooner I got down to some proper work the better. She also warned Alison that I had been brainwashed by the monks of the Society of the Sacred Mission (SSM), to whom she had been both mother and confessor in Basutoland. She explained that they had confused me with their silly notions about celibacy and wanted this sorted out because she knew monks to be a pathetic and unhappy lot.

It is only fair to say that I only heard of all this years later. However, looking back on it all now, it is clear that Alison had been given her orders and that, at least in some particulars, she carried them out to the letter. My grandmother also saw to it that Alison got to see the better side of Durban. While I was at work the next day, she took Alison on a tour of the magnificent beach hotels that had recently been erected in Umhlanga Rocks and to the new American-style shopping mall. She explained that she did not want Alison to leave with the impression that South Africa was a third world country and that I was bound only to show her Durban's shanty towns. My parents also did their bit by taking us out for a dinner dance at the prestigious Durban Country Club. My two brothers were embarrassingly polite. It was difficult to escape the uncomfortable feeling that an effort was being made by all the family.

On the third day of the visit, we stole away after dinner for a walk on the beach. By this time it was nearly dark and a full moon was rising over the sea, inviting us to walk out to it along a shining watery highway. It was a balmy, still evening and we took off our shoes and waded into the water. Africa was at her most bewitching and life could not be resisted. Alison took my hand and we stood silently watching the moon for what seemed a long time. Then we turned our back on the sea and walked into the shadow of a dune. There we briefly kissed for the first time, not entirely successfully because I had not fully made up my mind whether Alison was a welcome or a maddening distraction from the serious business for which I had returned to South Africa.

Despite my ambivalence about her visit, we spent two happy weeks together. Alison spotted some photographs on my grandmother's dressing table of me playing polo and asked to be shown how the game was played. This was not possible because polo is played in the South African winter. But her request provided a good pretext for spending some time on our own, so I drove her out to the deserted Inanda Polo Club, where I arranged for our groom to produce a horse. I knocked a ball around for a while and then dismounted and handed the horse back to the groom. Alison was clearly impressed, and asked in some awe, didn't I even tack up? Did the groom do everything? These questions were unexpected and a bit deflating after I had showed off my fine horsemanship. I was even more polite than usual to our groom and we walked the horse back with him to the stables. There we met his wife, who, on seeing Alison, put her hand to her mouth and said to me in

Sotho that Alison's hair was the colour of the fire under her cooking pot.

The only mishap took place while bathing in the sea and involved a runaway surfboard. This bore down on us as we were swimming at Ballito Bay, a resort north of Durban. Well used to the surf and aware of the danger of a surfboard's sharp tail fin, I dived deep under the wave only to come up to see Alison's head emerging from the swell with what looked like a red gash slicing down her forehead. My heart froze for an instant. Then she brushed the strand of red hair away and I started to breathe again. For a moment I thought I had lost this delicate English rose and was struck by the awesome responsibility of hosting her visit in a country where she was so clearly out of her depth.

We had stopped off en route to Bethesda, which I wanted to show Alison so that she could make up her own mind whether the rural African hospital was suitable for her medical elective. After our early morning swim, we continued up the Natal north coast, over the broad and muddy Tugela River, which the statesmanlike Cetswayho hoped would be respected as a natural southern boundary of his kingdom, and into a very different Zululand, now mostly owned by Whites and planted with sugar-cane. We passed Gingindhlovu, the place of the Elephant, one of the former royal kraals, passed the remains of the once vast Dunn reserve and, finally, having travelled for much of the day, climbed up into the Ubombo Mountains. The neat little hospital had sensibly been built in the foothills to provide relief from the stifling heat and malaria on the plain below.

The Medical Director, Daryl Hackland, was about to start his ward round when we arrived. He invited us to join him, an experience that provided me with my first glimpse into Alison's world of medicine. I emerged with a new respect for my English companion and all medical missionaries. The separate TB ward and the ward for malnourished children were especially pitiable. The smell of disinfectant was almost overpowering, and I found it a huge relief to emerge out into the open air to the scent of the frangipani trees, which, with foresight, had been planted over much of the site. Daryl then invited us back to his home for tea, where we met his wife, Priscilla, who had insisted on bringing her grand piano into the bush. She was delighted when Alison offered to play a tune and invited her to use it whenever she needed a break from medicine. With the grand piano, Bethesda was more than Alison had hoped for in an African hospital.

We went on from Bethesda to spend the night in a nearby Parks' Board chalet at Lake St Lucia. This was a cool rondavel, set under some mangrove trees close to the shore of the lake. I had not thought ahead to book us into a chalet with two separate rooms, and so when we were shown to a chalet with one room with separate beds, I was not sure what to do and how Alison would react. When she came in after me and made no comment, I lamely decided that the honourable thing to do was to give her a choice and offered to explore whether we could be moved to a chalet with two separate rooms. She responded wickedly that there was no need to bother as she was happy to risk sleeping in the same room with me. So risk it we did. It was a mistake, as I did not sleep a wink all night because the foreign presence under the bedclothes in the nearby bed was distinctly unsettling and I could not make up my mind whether my virtue had been challenged or an invitation had been extended to me.

On our way back to Durban, I drove Alison through one of Natal's two large game reserves, Hluhlwe. The other is the Umfolozi. Both are much smaller than South Africa's premier game reserve, the giant Kruger National Park, but they have all the main wild animals, the so-called big five: lion, elephant, cheetah, rhino and hippo. To our disappointment, we scarcely saw any game, save for some scattered herds of antelope. It was too hot for the animals to be out in the open. I had to promise Alison to take her to the Kruger on one of her next visits. The drive through the bushveldt was well worth it though, as it gave us some idea of what the early British settlers encountered when they settled Port Natal and then ventured into the interior on hunting and trading expeditions.

Our next adventure together took us south of Durban to meet Peter Moll, just released from detention barracks. Peter and his cousin Richard Steele, both Baptists, were the first conscripts from one of the mainline churches to refuse military service. I was looking forward to meeting him because I had followed his progress from afar for some time and hoped to gain a first-hand account of what was likely to lie in store for me.

Peter was recuperating at Hluleka on the Wild Coast, the beautifully rugged stretch of coast between Port Alfred and Port St John's. This coastal strip was then part of the Transkei, the traditional homeland of Nelson Mandela's tribe, the Xhosa. His forebears had migrated furthest south in the centuries' long migration of the Bantu people and then had been checked on the River Kei by the northward expansion of the Boer and British settlers from the Cape. After a period of considerable tension on this border caused by cattle rustling on both sides, the Xhosa committed national suicide in the 1850s, when the tribe recklessly followed a young prophetess, Nongqawusa. She called for the slaughter of all cattle as a sacrifice to the ancestors, who would then rise from the dead to drive the White settlers into the sea. Most believed her, did as she instructed and starved to death or were made destitute. With their power broken, the Transkei was declared a native reserve and administered as part of the Cape colony. While a disaster for the Xhosa, this decision preserved the virgin coastline from developers, and it remains today a haven for those looking for a simple beach holiday away from the high-rise hotels of mass tourism.

Peter met us with a wide grin, which was immediately reassuring as it suggested that he was none the worse for wear after his ordeal. Nevertheless, the account he gave of his experiences was sobering to say the least. After his one year sentence to detention barracks had been confirmed, he had been presented with a military uniform and ordered to wear it and report for punishment drill on the parade ground. Not unreasonably, having refused military service, he was not prepared to wear military uniform in DB. This Catch 22 meant that he could not avoid colliding time and again with the commanding officer, who insisted that all prisoners wore the same uniform. Each time he refused, he was summarily tried for refusing to obey a command and sentenced to the maximum period of fourteen days in solitary confinement in the punishment block. At the end of this period, he would be let out for a day, presented with the uniform, refuse and then be sentenced for another fourteen days. In all, Peter endured ten bouts of 'solitary'. He amusingly recalled how he earned a further fourteen days for being caught helping an inmate smuggle in a packet of cigarettes. Notwithstanding this one ignoble sentence, as I was later to discover, his endurance of a total of one hundred and fifty-four days of solitary confinement was an impressive feat of self-control.

There was a lot to ponder as Alison and I drove back after stopping over for a night with Peter's parents in their home in Umtata, the one-horse town and capital of the nominally independent Transkei. Our destination was Himeville, a village in the foothills of the Drakensberg Mountains, where my entire family was booked in to the small hotel for Christmas. Realising that I had neglected Alison, who complained that Peter and I had talked non-stop and that Peter had even joined us for what might have been a romantic late-night walk on the beach at Hluleka, I suggested we stop for a picnic lunch beside a mountain stream.

The sky was clear and the day was hot. We decorously took turns to put on our costumes behind the bushes and swam in the deliciously cool stream. While Alison continued swimming, I found a large rock to dry myself on and was able to watch as she emerged from the water. I closely observed her full figure for the first time and decided that it was really very fine. I also noticed how beautiful her pale skin was in the bright sunlight against the dark green of the riverbank. I, of course, could not help admiring her hair. I made up my mind that she would make a good African wife. When she looked up and caught me looking at her, she noticed that I was seeing her in another way. I detected a flash of triumph in her smile and in her eyes.

We later named the place 'White Lily' because there was a solitary white lily growing near the water's edge, and because we were then so pure. One of my regrets now is that we did not become lovers there and then. It was such a lovely place and we wasted so much time waiting. From this moment on, in her presence I was always aching for her like a musk elephant. But it could not have been otherwise. We were then both evangelical Christians from St Helen's for whom sex before marriage is unthinkable. So, even if we had considered the possibility, we could not have acted upon it. We had to wait and to endure a kind of prison. It was therefore a blessed release when the Christmas season ended.

Alison squeezed in her visit just in time, because shortly after she returned to medical school in England, I received a telephone call at Diakonia from a neighbour to warn me that two military policemen had just called at my parents' home and were on their way to arrest me. After taking the call, I tidied my desk as calmly as I could and then told Paddy. He summoned the multiracial staff of around twelve and told them what was about to happen. When the military police arrived, he invited the staff to join hands with me in the centre. This reception took the wind out of the policemen's sails and, much to my astonishment, they sheepishly joined the circle. After a short prayer, I was escorted from the building.

I was taken back home to collect a few personal things. There was a birthday card on the table for me from Alison, which I stealthily pocketed when the police were not looking. Then I was driven to the small military detention barracks in Durban North, where detainees were held overnight before being transferred to detention barracks proper in the vast military base at Voortrekkerhoogte, outside Pretoria. I was banged up in a cell, which had a mattress on the floor and a bucket in the corner. The barred window was too high to look out of. My only possessions were the clothes I was wearing. For the first time in my life, I really had lost all my freedom and all my privileges. It made for a curiously mixed feeling, part panic and part immense relief that what I had most dreaded was at last underway. Then the panic receded and was replaced by a profound sense of tiredness, which made me realise just how long I had been nervously anticipating this moment.

I was left alone for a few hours slumped on the mattress before something altogether surreal happened. My cell gate was unlocked and I was summoned to watch the week's prison entertainment, the cinematic masterpiece by Francis Ford Coppola, *Apocalypse Now*. The film's opening scenes have ever since been etched on my memory. They begin with a squadron of American combat helicopters appearing on a distant horizon, looking like large, black menacing vultures, which come steadily closer to the sound of Wagner's *Ride of the Valkyries*. When it is possible to make the helicopters out, they suddenly swoop down to attack a helpless Vietnamese village, dropping napalm and machine-gunning men, women and children hopelessly trying to flee the aerial assault. When the village is completely gutted, the helicopters fly back into the sunrise from which they came. The remainder of the film takes one deeper and deeper into the horror of a war from which all civilised values have been eliminated: a veritable heart of darkness.

After the first scenes, I dismissed the film as yet another 'skiet and donner' (shoot and kill) enjoyed by the sort of military enthusiast who played with toy soldiers as a boy. But then it slowly dawned on me that *Apocalypse Now* is a savage denunciation of the Vietnam War, and that the film might also have been made of the war I was being called upon to fight on South Africa's borders. Within hours of my arrest and detention, I could not have asked for anything more reassuring. I recall feeling strangely elated and took the film to be a 'sign' that I was, after all, in exactly the right place.

Alison's birthday card and enclosed letter also helped make the experience more bearable. After I had been locked up in my cell again and was confident that the prison was settling down for the night and that I would not be detected, I took the letter out and read it slowly, savouring every sentence, as a way of calming myself. She wrote, in her inimitable happy way of the gentle English countryside, the British weather, her delightful flatmates and of the debate in the Church of England about the ordination of women as priests. She also mentioned apprehensively her approaching examinations. Knowing something about the mad whirl of her life in London, which had appeared to me to leave very little time for medical studies, I realised that she had reason to be concerned and wondered if she would ever make it through to the medical elective stage, when she would be unleashed on real patients and, what was more, on my fellow countrymen and women.

I read the letter several times the following day on the steam train as it puffed along transporting me, under guard, from Durban to Pretoria. The first stop along the way was Pietermaritzburg station, very familiar to me because it was the end point of the long journey I used to make from Basutoland to my boarding school. Very touchingly a group of my friends working for Scripture Union in the Private Schools were waiting on the platform to support me, and my guard allowed me off the train to briefly greet them. As we resumed the journey, I was reminded that Pietermaritzburg station was famous as the station where Mahatma Gandhi, then practising as a barrister in Durban after being called to the bar in England, was evicted from a first class carriage for being Black. The incident was to change the direction of Gandhi's life by settling the question of who he was – an Englishman or an Indian. From this time on he started to campaign for an end to racism against his fellow Indians in South Africa and to develop the philosophy of non-violent direct action or *satyagraha*, which was to influence the ANC's non-violent defiance campaign against apartheid in the 1950s, under its President and Nobel Peace Prize winner, Chief Albert Luthuli. As a disciple of both Mahatma Gandhi and Albert Luthuli, I silently saluted the place where the Great Soul was so unceremoniously hauled off the train, and prayed for some of his courage.

When the train finally chugged into Pretoria, I could not help wryly remembering the last time I visited the gracious jacaranda tree-lined administrative capital of South Africa. It was to captain the Natal schools' rugby team in a curtain raiser to the test match between the Springboks and the British Lions in 1974 at Loftus Versveld, the heart of South African rugby. At the end of the match, we lined up at the entrance to clap on the two test teams and watched in awe as sporting legends such as Willie John McBride, Gareth Edwards and J.P.R. Williams ran on to the field. Now, barely seven years later, South Africa had become such a pariah state that no international team would dare play its all-White national teams. While this denied some of the world's finest athletes and sportsmen and sportswomen international competition, the sports boycott counted more to the man in the street than the arms embargo or economic sanctions.

There would be lots of time for memories of heroic moments and daydreams of more to come. But as it turned out, my arrest was a muddle. Evidently copies of the letter I had sent from London and the one I had sent on my return had not been passed from the high command in Pretoria to the regiment in Natal, where I had been ordered to report for military training. As a result, when I failed to turn up, the regiment had sent its military police to find and arrest me and, without any attempt at concealment on my part, they must have been searching for me for the best part of two years. By the time the train reached Pretoria, a letter from a solicitor, whom Paddy had engaged on my behalf, had arrived and explained that I had written to the SADF to request a trial and therefore was not the fugitive from justice my regiment took me to be. The upshot of it all was that, no sooner had I set foot in the dreaded detention barracks at Voortrekkerhoogte, than I was discharged on notice that I would be recalled at some indeterminate future time to face court martial. There was nothing for me to do but to get back on the train, return to Durban and keep waiting.

When I turned up unexpectedly for work at Diakonia the following day, my new friends, who had seen me off in the custody of the military police barely four days before, were a little nonplussed but not greatly surprised. They put it down to the power of their prayers and the inefficiency of the apartheid system, which all endured with good humour and an infinite patience. Although I was able to return to work as if nothing had happened and was pleased that my brief detention had given me a kind of dummy run for the real thing, it had shaken me up a bit and impressed on me that my days of freedom were numbered.

My adventures at large though were not yet over. I discovered that the post of Diocesan Secretary and Treasurer of the Anglican Diocese of Namibia had fallen vacant and decided to apply in order to see something of South Africa's war on Namibia's border with Angola. I also thought that entering the war zone in Namibia as an unarmed civilian would help counter the charge of cowardice I expected would be made against me at my forthcoming court martial. I duly applied and was accepted at the princely salary of R200 per month, which my father objected would not keep him in whisky for a week.

5

WAR ZONE

I, the Great General of the German soldiers, address this letter to the
Herero people. The Herero are no longer considered German
subjects . . . Within the German boundaries, every Herero, whether
found armed or unarmed, . . . will be shot.

The Great General of the Mighty Kaiser, Lothar von Trotha

The scramble for a slice of the African cake in the late nineteenth century produced some very unlikely colonies. None
more so than German South West Africa or what is now called
Namibia. Except for the remote northern part, the country is
nearly all desert or semi-desert. Its so-called Skeleton Coast is
well named, for many a ship has run aground with little hope
of the survivors making it back, along miles and miles of
unbroken coastline, to the main port of Walvis Bay.

I flew into Windhoek airport to take up my new post on 1
March 1981. The road leading to the old German capital was
lined by grotesque-looking stunted plants. It was so hot that
the tarmacadam had melted and was sticking to car tyres. I
could not help thinking that David Livingstone, the renowned
missionary doctor, who opened up the interior of Africa over
a period of thirty years of exploration, and called for
Christianity, commerce and civilisation to save the African
from the slave trade, must have been especially convincing to

persuade the Germans to take on Namibia as a sacred trust. Either that, or something made them believe that Eldorado was beneath all that sand.

The colony was not a success from the start. The Germans, with none of the experience of the British, Portuguese, or Dutch in Africa, were soon at loggerheads with the inhabitants for trying to put an end to the cattle-thieving between the Namas, who lived to the south of Windhoek, and the Herero, who lived to the north. The competition between German settlers and local tribesmen for scarce grazing land and the contemptuous behaviour of the settlers towards the natives further aggravated tensions in the colony until they flared into open revolt. The Herero, a striking people who adopted the dress of Rhenish missionaries sent to Christianise them, led the uprising. Troop reinforcements were rushed in from Germany and the ruthless General Lothar von Trotha was put in charge of pacifying the natives. The campaign was brutal and any Herero who surrendered were placed in labour camps, where over half were estimated to have died.

In 1904, von Trotha went a step further and virtually exterminated the remaining mutinous Herero by positioning his troops in such a way that he deliberately drove men, women, children, and their cattle into the waterless Omaheke sandveld. When the stragglers were through he ordered his troops to seal the last waterhole and issued an order that the Herero were no longer the Kaiser's subjects and, should any attempt to return to their former lands, they would be shot. His edict made it clear that he would not accept the return of women and children. Some 8000 men, with many more women and children, and all their cattle and horses were trapped. A few made it through the desert to the Cape and Bechuanaland but most died of thirst and starvation. Those who tried to break back were bayoneted or shot.

With such an experience of colonisation, there was understandable rejoicing in Namibia when the First World War ended in the defeat of the Kaiser and the confiscation of all

German colonies. In 1919, the newly formed League of Nations, with the former Boer military commander and internationally respected statesman Jan Smuts as one of its leading architects, gave South Africa a mandate over South West Africa until the country was ready to take control of its own affairs. The change did not have any appreciable impact on the lives of ordinary Namibians because the South Africans were to prove equally careless about how many they killed as part of their subjugation of the territory. The main difference was that, whereas the Germans had largely kept to the southern and central part of the country, the South Africans concentrated their efforts on the Ovambo people, who lived in the remote north and provided most of the recruits for the guerrilla movement, the South West African People's Organisation (SWAPO).

As happened in South Africa, SWAPO started out as a Black political party that was forced into exile. The country's Nelson Mandela, Herman Ja Toivo, along with other resistance leaders, was arrested, tortured in Pretoria Central Prison, and sentenced in 1968 to life imprisonment on Robben Island with Mandela. Like the ANC, the guerrilla movement set up bases in neighbouring countries, from where it mounted hit and run raids on South African forces stationed along the border of Namibia and Angola. Much of the internal opposition to South Africa's occupation had been suppressed. Several church leaders had been deported, including two former expatriate bishops of the Anglican Church, Colin Winter and Richard Woods, and the diocese's Vicar General, Edward Morrow. They had been guilty of supporting the cause of Namibian independence and of drawing attention to South Africa's illegal occupation of Namibia in terms of international law.

In support of their claim, they had drawn on advisory opinions of the World Court and on several United Nations resolutions. The most important of these, Resolution 2145, was passed in 1967 after Ja Toivo and other Namibian leaders were taken into custody under the Terrorism Act. It terminated

South Africa's mandate and set up a Council for Namibia to administrate the territory until it became independent. In 1969, the Security Council of the United Nations supported the call for South Africa to withdraw and, when South Africa showed no intention of complying, declared the occupation illegal. In 1971, the World Court supported this ruling and insisted that South Africa should withdraw from Namibia immediately.

But it was all of no avail. Ten years later, it was clear to all that South Africa had no intention of relinquishing control, as the original mandate had envisaged. South African troops moved freely about Windhoek, which, with its solid Lutheran churches and beer gardens, had the exotic feel of a European city. My new office was based near the Anglican Cathedral, a reassuringly traditional-looking English village church. Beyond the peaceful city centre is the bustling Katatura Township, with its Tukondjeni market, where one can buy omaungu, a kind of dried spinach, and, among other local delicacies, mopane worms. It was a very African market, with fashionable ladies at every corner having their hair braided and coiled, groups of men playing card games and dice, and little boys running about driving their model cars made out of spare pieces of wire

I had barely moved in before I was asked to drive the Bishop, James Kauluma, the nearly thousand miles from the capital to Ovamboland, where over half the population lives on a giant flood plain of the Cunene River. It was explained to me that he needed a driver because this former Ovambo herdsman had only recently learned to drive, had written off three large expensive vehicles donated by rich, sympathetic Americans, and therefore should not drive the long journey on his own. The terrifying part of the experience was when the bishop insisted on sharing some of the driving. He would take the wheel, hunch over it and proceed to drive at a snail's pace with rapt concentration and in total silence. The tension was almost unbearable and I suspect his accidents were caused by a slip of concentration brought on by an inability to relax.

Despite his atrocious driving, James Kauluma was a very good Bishop of Damaraland, as the Anglican Diocese of Namibia was then called. After South Africa's deportations had made the diocese leaderless, he had been summoned from postgraduate study in the United States to be consecrated bishop in St Paul's Cathedral, London. I grew increasingly fond of him on our long journeys, especially after an incident alerted me to just how rife racism was in Namibia. At the end of a particularly long stretch of road, we pulled up outside a café in one of the small towns. I suggested we go in and buy some refreshments, to which Bishop James responded that he would wait in the car. On entering the café, I noticed that there were two distinct compartments, with Whites on the one side and Blacks on the other. Had we walked in together, the first Namibian bishop, who was married to a White American and had earned a Masters in Theology from an American university, faced a humiliating confrontation with a totally undistinguished White shopkeeper. Perhaps wisely, he decided that this particular battle was not worth fighting when the war we would encounter at the end of our journey presented a far greater challenge for him and his people.

I also came to respect the way he dealt fairly but firmly with every part of his far-flung diocese. On one occasion, for instance, we arrived unexpectedly at one of the church's rural schools, on the last day of term, to find the children had been sent home a day early. On finding no good reason for their early departure, he admonished the teachers for not fulfilling their duty to educate the children for a full term and promptly deducted a day's salary from each of the teachers' pay cheques. As treasurer, I was called on there and then to write out the new cheques, which the teachers accepted with good grace. They too were fond of their bishop.

Our forays into Ovamboland were always a risky affair. It was a war zone strewn with landmines. The South African military had taken a strategic decision to try and contain SWAPO by creating a wide no-man's-land along the border and by forcing SWAPO to operate from bases deep inside Angola. As a result, both sides waged war by mounting cross-border hit-and-run raids. The occasional SWAPO infiltration was a suicide mission because, with South African spotter planes ceaselessly patrolling the border, it was virtually impossible for the guerrillas to strike a target in Namibia and then escape back to base in Angola without detection. The grisly progress of the manhunts launched to cut them off would be reported daily on the lunchtime news. I recall being sickened by the triumphant tone of a newscaster reporting on the final sighting and elimination of one of these guerrilla bands.

Travel in this area was also dangerous on account of the notorious South African police counter-insurgency unit *Koevoet*, which translated from the Afrikaans means crowbar. As the South African Minister of Law and Order, Louis le Grange, explained, its purpose was to be the 'crowbar which prises terrorists out of the bushveld like nails from rotten wood'. T-shirts worn by off-duty members that proclaimed 'Murder is our business – and business is good' suggests something about the unit's methods. New recruits were trained at Vlakplaas, a remote farm in the Transvaal, where they were allegedly required to kidnap an innocent Black civilian from the nearby township at dead of night, bring them back to Vlakplaas, torture them in front of their comrades for entertainment and then kill them. While the full extent of their activities will never be proven, the collapse of the case the government brought against Archbishop Hurley in 1984 for publicly claiming that Koevoet was responsible for atrocities, strongly supports numerous allegations that the unit was responsible for some of the worst violence of the apartheid era.

As in all guerrilla warfare, where unarmed guerrillas and civilians are impossible to distinguish, the main battle was fought for the hearts and minds of the people. SWAPO needed civilians as cover, while the SADF needed civilians to identify the guerrillas hiding among them. One of Koevoet's favourite tactics was to undermine popular support for SWAPO by attacking civilians while disguised as SWAPO guerrillas. One of these raids is held to have laid waste the Anglican mission of St Mary, Odibo, formerly one of the country's leading educational institutions. In the raid, a large party of schoolchildren were abducted and have not been heard of since. When the bishop and I arrived to inspect what was left of the mission, we found the classrooms empty of children, the floors of the clinic littered with broken medical equipment and shattered bottles of medicine, and its large reservoir, which used to provide an essential supply of clean water, cracked and beyond repair. I left the bishop talking to the lonely caretaker and wandered amongst the silent ruins trying to imagine it with all the schoolchildren, teachers, seminarians, priests, doctors, nurses and patients, and thinking what its closure must have meant to the missionaries who had made it their life's work.

Not only is a guerrilla war devastating for the civilian population caught in the crossfire but it also has a disproportionate impact on women. Men of combatant age in the war zone are always suspect: if they are not combatants, then why not? With Koevoet roaming about the countryside in their armoured cars picking up anyone who looked remotely suspicious and then submitting them to a brutal interrogation, men of combatant age tried to make themselves invisible. Those who did not join SWAPO journeyed to the south in search of work as migrant labourers, leaving the women to work the land and to take the full brunt of Koevoet. The absence of the men also meant that it was the women who hid and fed the guerrillas and had to bear the consequences when they were found out. It was estimated that there were at least two women to every man in Ovamboland by the end of the war. Those hospitals that remained open recorded a steady stream of rapes, unwanted pregnancies and new-born children abandoned on the doorstep. For me, the most disturbing experience of my time in the war zone was a visit to an isolated homestead near St Mary's with Bishop James and the local pastor to console a woman who had been left unprotected and had recently been beaten and repeatedly raped, allegedly by members of Koevoet.

St Mary's, Odibo, was the closest I was to come to the war South Africa was waging in Namibia. Later at my court martial, against the claim that the South African Defence Force was waging a defensive war in Namibia, I was able to point out that the United Nations had revoked South Africa's mandate and had declared its continuing occupation illegal. But even more important for me than this legal claim, was to have witnessed, at first hand, the cruelty and wastefulness of a war that was being mainly fought against civilians, and especially female civilians. This strengthened my resolve that I should on no account serve in the armed forces in any circumstances whatsoever, even in a non-combatant capacity as a medical orderly. This option was always a strong temptation because it would avoid the consequences of an outright refusal to serve and would avoid the possibility of being called upon to kill. But after seeing the destruction wrought by the presence of South African forces in Namibia, I reasoned that even a non-combatant role would provide indirect support for the war effort and amount to a betrayal of all those who had given their lives to bring education, healing and a future at Odibo.

Other than mourn its former glory, there was little to do at St Mary's and so the bishop and I moved on to visit local congregations in the area. Each stop became longer and longer as the bishop relaxed in the company of his people and enjoyed their hospitality, particularly the traditional fermented beer made from the fruit of the Hyphaene palm trees. I always had my eye on the clock on account of my responsibility to get James Kauluma through the military checkpoint on the road back to Windhoek before the curfew at 6 p.m. As the hour drew steadily nearer, I virtually had to drag the bishop away and into the car. We would then make a dash for it at high speed. We once drove at a reckless 120 m.p.h. over a stretch of road where a large kudu might have crossed the road around any corner, and even then arrived ten minutes late. Luckily, the police waived us through and we did not have to spend the night in the car.

On one visit to the north, we took a detour to take in the Etosha Pan nature reserve. The pan, an inland ocean of white salt and sand, is one of the natural wonders of the world and is thought to have been part of a lake that stretched all the way to the Okavango delta in neighbouring Botswana. For months and even years it remains dry. Then, when the heavy summer rainclouds come and break over the pan, it is transformed into a network of smaller pans and watercourses, which attract pink clouds of flamingoes to feed on the salty algal soup. Herds of zebra, wildebeest, springbok, gemsbok and giraffe appear as if from nowhere. When we visited, the rains had not fallen and the South African military had turned Etosha into their private shooting reserve, killing off many of the animals. Nevertheless we saw a large herd of elephant and a male lion in his prime.

My travels with Bishop James also took me to the Skeleton Coast, which boasts the highest sand-dunes in the world. The pretext was to visit some of the scattered Anglican congregations in this sparsely populated area and the Mission to Seamen, based at the fishing port of Walvis Bay. On the way we passed through the Namib Desert, the world's oldest unchanged desert. Eventually we emerged at the coast, with its year-round layer of mist caused by the freezing cold Atlantic waters. The coastline is potentially the world's richest pelagic fishing grounds, but had been severely over-fished by the South African- and European-owned fishing fleets in anticipation of their licences being revoked by an independent Namibian government.

This barren coastline also has some of the richest alluvial diamond fields in the world. The diamond deposits had also been over-exploited as a hedge against a future hostile government. In this case, such was the international outrage, that the United Nations passed Decree 1 in 1974, a measure intended to prevent foreign interests from exploiting

Namibia's natural resources. However, by the time of my visit, the depletion of these natural resources had progressed so far that the once fashionable port of Lüderitz, a thriving fishing port and a centre of the diamond mining industry in the sixties and seventies, was in sad decline. It was almost a ghost town on its way to becoming another Kolmanskop, a town further along the coast, where sand covers the streets and has entered into the hallways of its once fine German-style buildings.

On our return journey through the Namib Desert, we stopped off to meet a senior lay Anglican working as general manager of the Rossing uranium mine. The mine was controversial for several reasons. The majority shareholder of the mine, the British mining giant, Rio Tinto Zinc, was accused of mining illegally in Namibia in contravention of Decree 1. Western governments, mainly those of France and Britain, which bought Namibian uranium, were accused of being in breach of the United Nations resolution. Meanwhile, South Africa, without oil and uranium reserves of its own, was intent on developing an advanced nuclear energy industry to beat the international oil embargo on the back of Namibian uranium. Furthermore, after an American spy satellite detected what had all the marks of a nuclear explosion in the Atlantic Ocean in 1977, it was thought highly likely that South Africa had developed its own nuclear bomb using enriched uranium mined in Namibia. Recognising its political significance, SWAPO orchestrated a strike at the mine in 1979, making it a focus of industrial relations unrest in the country. All this background made our meeting with the general manager a delicate affair. I could not help pitying him for the weight of moral responsibility he carried.

It was not long after our excursion to the Skeleton Coast that I received an invitation to lunch from a South African conscript serving his military service in the legal corps of the occupying army. He had attended a service at the Anglican Cathedral in Windhoek and, as we knew each other from the University of Natal, had noticed me in the congregation. I was not entirely happy with fraternising with a South African dressed in military uniform in Namibia but decided that it would be churlish to refuse a fellow Christian. In the course of our meeting I was rash enough to enquire what, as a trained lawyer, he thought of the legality of South Africa's military presence in Namibia. The question did not go down well because a fortnight later I received a summons from the legal department of the South African Defence Force to appear before a court martial in one month's time at Voortrekkerhoogte.

My time in 'Suidwes', as White South Africans still like to call the territory they regarded as their fiefdom, was up. I finished off the annual financial accounts of the Diocese of Damaraland and, as a memento of Namibia, bought a characterful lino-print by John Muafengejo, the Namibian artist. The one I chose for Alison was of a large, nubile Ovambo woman, with huge buttocks and ample bosom, and an inscription beneath which translates from the Ovambo, 'God made love good'. After buying this print, John urged me to help myself to a pile of others that he claimed were unfinished and that he would never get round to finishing. I declined because I felt I ought to pay for them and my church salary did not extend to more than one. It was probably my costliest mistake ever because John died some years later and I came across his prints at an exhibition in London's Barbican gallery, where the cheapest was selling for £10,000.

6

COURT MARTIAL

It has struck me as one of the oddities of our country that some
of its most outstanding leaders have had some connection to
Robben Island. By a strange coincidence Archbishop Hurley
too spent a few years on the island.
His father was a lighthouse keeper.

(Archbishop Desmond Tutu in *Denis Hurley, A Portrait by Friends*)

It would be nice to recall my trial as a dazzling display of
eloquence, passion and fearlessness. Nelson Mandela's closing
speech at the Rivonia treason trial springs to mind as the kind
of oratory that I would like to have matched. The reality of
my court martial was altogether different and I cannot now
suppress more than a tinge of embarrassment reflecting on
what I said and how I conducted myself. I now wish I had been
more prepared and thought it through more. It was a public
occasion after all and presented an opportunity to say things
about apartheid and war which should have been better said.

My biggest mistake is that I did not speak from the heart
and simply say that apartheid was morally indefensible. I
should then have added my strongest legal argument that to
wage war in Namibia was to participate in an illegal act
because, in terms of international law, South Africa was in
illegal occupation. I could have added that, as none of South

Africa's neighbours had declared war on South Africa, it was also wrong for me to participate in a so-called Defence Force that was known to be supporting rebel forces in both Angola and Mozambique.

I need not and should not have said another word. Instead, my trial dragged on over two days and at times descended into total farce. This started outside the courtroom, where I waited for the summons to enter, with two uniformed guards on either side of me. As I had travelled by train from Windhoek to Pretoria and had no formal clothes with me for the trial, I had relied on my mother to bring me something suitable from the small wardrobe of clothes I had left in Durban. For some unfathomable reason, she brought a loud check sports coat. I wished I had given her instructions to bring my dark suit because the sports coat not only made me feel ridiculous but I also feared that this quintessentially English garment sent out all the wrong signals to a court bound to be divided between English and Afrikaans speakers and where, given their long history, any Englishman appearing before an Afrikaans court was in a kind of double jeopardy: one, for having possibly committed an offence and, two, for being English.

All this flashed through my mind before the summons came. When it did, the two young guards in military uniform snapped to attention on either side of me. They expected me to march in with them, which, in my sports coat, would have made me look even more of a goon. I had also decided to insist at every point that I was a civilian and not a soldier. So I let the guards march in ahead of me and walked after them at a steady pace with what dignity I could muster. When I had caught up with them, they saluted the President of the Court, who dismissed them, leaving me standing alone in the centre of the courtroom. It was an awkward moment and I involuntary clasped my hands behind my back, as an English gentleman does when he is not quite sure of himself.

The courtroom was divided as I had expected. The President of the Court, Colonel P.J. de Klerk, from the wings on his uniform, was an officer in the air force. The prosecutor was a thickset young lawyer from the army's legal department, who sat with a team of assistants. Their accents betrayed them as Afrikaners. Opposite sat my defence, which had been arranged for me by supporters, about seventy of whom were in attendance. They had engaged the brilliant human rights lawyer, Christopher Nicholson. Despite the outcome of the trial being a foregone conclusion, he was determined to put as strong a legal case as possible and to this end asked a senior counsel, Andrew Wilson, to argue the case. To provide expert witness on the Church's teaching on war, he invited two of South Africa's most senior churchmen, the President of the Southern African Catholic Bishops' Conference, Archbishop Denis Hurley, and the Anglican Archbishop elect of Cape Town, Philip Russell. The third expert witness was Professor John Dugard, the renowned South African authority on international law. All three distinguished witnesses were English-speaking South Africans.

The going was tough from the start and I made it more difficult for myself than it might have been by basing my refusal to serve, not only on the injustice of apartheid and the illegality of South Africa's occupation of Namibia, but also on the grounds of Christian pacifism. In retrospect, this was a bad mistake, because it gave the prosecution an opportunity to play down the issues of injustice and illegality that my defence raised, and to concentrate their attack on a much softer target. Furthermore my pacifist stance forced the two archbishops to concede that pacifism is a minority teaching within both the Roman Catholic and Anglican churches, and to admit that both their churches allow Christians to fight in a just war. This is a war that passes the test of just cause, is waged as a last resort, has a reasonable chance of success, the immunity of non-combatants is respected, and the use of force is proportionate. Despite the reasonableness of these criteria, I was unwilling to accept the just war theory for three main practical reasons.

Firstly, far from limiting the frequency and ferocity of war, my reading of Church history suggested that just war theory was seldom, if ever, rigorously applied and tended to be exploited by alliances between church and state to baptise war when this suited. The pathetic spectacle of the European nations decimating their youth in the trench warfare of the First World War, only leaving off the slaughter to sing hymns together on Christmas day, provides a good example.

Secondly, when I placed myself in the shoes of a South African or Namibian freedom fighter and asked myself what just war theory required of them, I concluded that, on account of the overwhelming firepower of the South African armed forces, it would require them to lay down their arms because a guerrilla war was not winnable. But this conclusion denied the value of the heroic sacrifices made by the SWAPO and ANC guerrillas who had given their lives in an attempt to liberate their respective countries. While I believed it was wrong for me to fight, I could not accept that what they had done was wrong.

Third and lastly, I held that the threat of human extinction posed by the development of nuclear weapons has vindicated the pacifist tradition with its absolute prohibition against war as a means of settling national and international disputes. Considering that the United States, a society at the vanguard of civilisation, had actually used these weapons, I argued that this threat was real and that it made the adoption of non-violent means of resolving conflict imperative. I might have added that, with South Africa suspected of possessing nuclear weapons, and with the Cold War being fought on African soil, it was not beyond the bounds of possibility that the conflict in Southern Africa could escalate to include the use of weapons of mass destruction.

In addition to these practical reasons for rejecting just war theory, I claimed that Christian pacifism can be traced to the earliest Christian communities. I pointed out that service in the Roman army was prohibited for Christians on the understanding that they should not kill because Christ had suffered and died for all people. As the early fourth-century martyr

Martin of Tours professed, 'I am Christ's soldier, I cannot fight.' I also drew on a paper by James Moulder, a philosopher at the University of Natal, which analysed the example of Jesus in relation to war and concluded that the Christian disciple should not serve as a combatant in war because it is impossible to picture Christ, the Redeemer, Healer and Teacher, killing the people he came to heal and to save.

Twenty years on, having shed, with some regret, the bright innocence of youth, I recognise that war presents a more complex challenge to the Christian conscience than I was prepared to admit. But that is now. Then I was faced with the difficult task of defending a strict Christian pacifism as part of a wider objection to military service in the South African Defence Force against a hostile prosecution determined to exploit the one weak link in my defence. The cross-examination seemed to go on and on. The questions fired at me became more and more pointed with the clear intention of entrapping me by both exposing the weaknesses of the strict pacifist position and by making the case that I was not really a religious objector at all but rather was politically motivated.

At one point the judge intervened and asked me what I would do if Idi Amin, the notorious Ugandan dictator, sent a squadron to bomb South African civilians. There was of course no answer to this kind of question. Replace Idi Amin with Hitler and it was the trump card used against conscientious objectors in the Second World War. Faced by such monstrous evil, I hope I would have responded by finding some way to oppose the root cause of the evil, like the pacifist, who was not a strict pacifist, Dietrich Bonhoeffer. But I understood that to concede something along these lines would be construed by the court as a repudiation of pacifism, so I replied that it was a hypothetical situation, which I had not considered. I went on to say that in the actual situation that faced me, I could only repeat that I found apartheid to be indefensible and that the war in Namibia was illegal.

The Anglican Archbishop-elect, Philip Russell, followed on

from me in the witness stand. He was a short, trim figure, with a brisk, businesslike manner, who had been awarded the MBE for bomb disposal work in the Second World War. He declared himself satisfied that I had taken the trouble to inform my conscience by my reading of the Church's teaching on war and by my experience of life under apartheid in South Africa and in Namibia. He explained that the Anglican Church did not forbid its members to serve in the South African Defence Force but supported their right to refuse to do so, and insisted that, when there is a conflict between Church and State, the Christian is compelled to obey his conscience for 'disobedience to conscience is sin'. When challenged by the President of the Court whether widespread conscientious objection might undermine the capacity of the state to defend itself against unChristian forces, which might eradicate the things Christ stood for, he displayed some of the qualities that had made him expert in the defusing of bombs. He coolly replied that Christianity thrives under persecution and that 'ultimately the Church of God is unconquerable'.

Archbishop Hurley's great learning and moral authority came to my aid next. Taking the witness stand, he addressed the unspoken issue at the centre of my trial: the fear of the White minority. He pointed out that lasting security can only be founded on social justice. He then explained that, even though the Church had agonised over the human instinct for self-preservation and had concluded that there is a natural right to self-defence, the teaching of Christ is thoroughly in favour of non-violence. He went on to point out that the right to self-defence was imported into Christianity whereas non-violence came from Christ himself. Furthermore, supporting my argument about the abuse of just war theory, he held that 'the right of self-defence has been misused so often, that today the teaching of the Church is to support and lift up those standing for non-violence. Their role is a prophetic one. It is compatible with the abolition of slavery. This was achieved because the Christian idealists relentlessly pursued their convictions. Some of the greatest progress in human history has come from individuals who felt that they could not bring themselves to accept laws which conflicted with their conscience.' In closing, he hoped that faith would replace fear because 'obedience to Christ's teaching and trust in God's providence will produce far more good than will insistence on the right of self-defence'.

At the end of his testimony, Colonel de Klerk challenged Archbishop Hurley to say whether my statement that the apartheid policy is indefensible was correct. This was a leading question because making statements which 'recommend, encourage, aid, instigate or suggest' to any person liable for national service that they should refuse or fail to render service was a heavily punishable offence in terms of section 121 of the Defence Act. Doubtless aware of the consequences of what he was doing, the archbishop replied cautiously that 'the accused has every right to put forward the views that he has. To imply that these views are purely political is unfair, because political views are always based on a religious or moral belief and therefore flow from conscience. No man is ever required to submit conscience to the state. To do so is totalitarian, as in Marxism. It is sinful.' Then he declared unflinchingly and bluntly, 'Yes, in the light of how apartheid has worked in the last thirty years, I would consider that his judgement that apartheid is indefensible to be the judgement of an informed conscience.'

Professor John Dugard then took the witness stand to contribute two vital legal points to my defence. The first supported my view that South Africa's occupation of Namibia was illegal in international law. From his knowledge and wide contacts in this field of law, he said with authority that it 'is a reasonable and widely held position' that South Africa's presence in Namibia was illegal. The second provided a legal basis for my refusal to serve in the SADF, which was the *de facto* military power in Namibia, in the natural law school of thought, which holds that if a law sinks below certain moral standards it is to be disregarded. He explained that this school of law provided the basis for convicting Nazi war criminals in the Nuremberg Trials and that South Africa had given support to the London Charter that established these trials. He thereby made the legal point that a South African court of law need not feel itself bound to uphold South African law in this case because the law had sunk below an acceptable moral standard by seeking to force me to commit acts which constituted a war crime.

With the full moral and legal implications of all that was at stake in my refusal of military service ringing in all our ears, the president adjourned the court until the following day to consult with his assessors. We shall never know whether they realised just how much they were in the dock after Professor Dugard raised the spectre of the Nuremberg Trials, but he must have given them pause for thought because the long statement read at the close of the trial suggests that they spent most of the night drafting its wording. For me, the respite from the courtroom drama, with its relentless questioning, provided a welcome opportunity to thank my supporters and defence team, to speak briefly at a vigil held at St George's church in Parktown, Johannesburg, and to enjoy a meal alone with my parents. My dear Mum and Dad were, if anything, even more overwhelmed at all that was happening than I was. To their credit, while neither of them had supported my initial refusal to undergo military training, they now stood fullsquare behind me at a time when many of their peers thought I was 'letting the side down'.

When we assembled outside the court the following morning, Archbishop Hurley was especially supportive of me. By this time, the two of us had walked a long way on this particular road together. Just before the summons, he drew me aside and prepared me for what was to come with his characteristic warmth and gentle humour. He said, 'I have asked the nuns to pray and when they pray nothing can withstand them.' As before, and as he had done for so many others, he was able to still the storm of apartheid then raging about me and to impart the courage to go on.

Thankfully the charade of a trial was quickly over in the morning. Either the cat had played for long enough with its mouse, or the embarrassing support I had received from my three distinguished witnesses had decided Colonel de Klerk that there was nothing further to be gained from dragging proceedings out. Ignoring Professor Dugard's assertion that I was not bound by South African law because it had sunk below an acceptable level, de Klerk ruled that the South African Defence Act provided only one absolute exemption from military service in terms of section 71, which was medical unfitness and that it otherwise imposed an unqualified obligation in unqualified terms. He concluded that, in spite of finding 'the accused does in fact sincerely believe and is bound by conscience not to take part in military activity or the SADF', he was therefore bound to find me guilty of refusing military service.

De Klerk then asked my defence to plead in mitigation of sentence. Andrew Wilson rose and argued that it would be inappropriate for me to be sentenced to a military prison because I had refused military service. He explained that I was bound to refuse military dress and discipline in detention barracks, which would pose further difficulties for both the military and me. As a way of avoiding these, he recommended that the court should explore imposing a fine. But, if the court decided that a custodial sentence was appropriate, he entered the plea that I should be treated as a civilian, as I had requested, and be sent to civilian prison.

After a short recess to consider the plea, Colonel de Klerk reconvened the court to pass sentence. Dressed in his smart military uniform, with his 'wings' proudly displayed on his epaulettes, the silence was palpable as he rose to read the following prepared statement:

'The court has taken account of all the facts especially:
1. You are young, a first offender who can be recharged so that

this may not be the end of the road. The penalties stated in Sec. 126A (2 years or R2000 fine or both) are the maximum penalties. You have made a good impression on the court. You are subjectively honest in your opinion and that opinion is based on a Christian attitude. You have discharged the onus on you to prove this, as far as that goes. You are intelligent and knew the risks involved in this course of action. The court accepts that the sentence may have a corrective effect.

2. The court has to consider the times in which we live. A military onslaught is being made on our borders and possibly inside them. If those attacking us were only nationalists it would not be so bad. But there is also tremendous pressure from Marxist and non-Christian sources. It is a serious *de facto* situation. Without making too much of it, you have shared your place with strange and dangerous bedmates, people who sin against God.

3. The court has to take account of parity of treatment. National servicemen do two years and some camps, which may be extended. Some give their lives and are maimed. It is a hard and serious situation in which this sentence has to be weighed.

4. We have to ponder the situation of the Government. No Government claims perfection. They are subject to practical strictures and are doing their best. There are historical and other factors, social and financial implications. A court of law cannot sit in judgement on the legislature.

5. We have to take account of your attitude. You may be living in an ivory tower, a young man who is a bit inexperienced.

6. There are other people in your situation and similar attitudes have to be discouraged.

The court is not prepared to impose a fine. R50 is inappropriate. We also do not want to send someone of your background and attitude and a first offender to gaol. The only other sentence is detention. You are sentenced to 12 months in Detention Barracks.'

All but the final sentence in the long statement washed over me. I barely had the time to hand my loud check sports coat back to my mother before being whisked off to detention barracks.

7

DETENTION BARRACKS

I write it out in a verse –
MacDonagh and MacBride
And Connolly and Pearse
Now and in time to be,
Wherever green is worn,
Are changed, changed utterly:
A terrible beauty is born.

(William Butler Yeats, 'Easter 1916')

Far away in Northern Ireland, Irish Republican Army prisoners were staging a hunger strike in the Maze prison. They understood themselves to be engaged in a war of independence and were protesting at the British refusal to grant them prisoner of war status. The protest had started with the prisoners refusing to wear the prison uniform. When the authorities responded by not allowing them to 'slop out' until they were properly clothed, the protest escalated into a dirty one. They smeared excrement on the walls of their cells in order not to have to stand in it. When successive negotiations between the leadership of the Roman Catholic Church and Sinn Féin, the Irish Republican political movement, and the British government failed, the prisoners resorted to hunger strike. The British Prime Minister, Margaret Thatcher, was adamant that she would not negotiate with terrorists, even though the hunger strikers' leader, Bobby Sands, was elected a Member of Parliament while he lay on his deathbed in the prison hospital. He died on Tuesday 5 May 1981.

It was in these uncompromising days that I started my sentence on Tuesday 12 May 1981, exactly a week after the death of Bobby Sands. I was initially placed in an isolated block of cells kept for prisoners whose sentences were awaiting confirmation. The process usually took three to four days, during which time prisoners were allowed to retain their civilian clothes and were not required to perform punishment drill on the parade ground. I was so exhausted by the nervous energy expended on my trial that I slept solidly for most of the three days. On the third day I was paid a visit by the Director of Military Law, Brigadier C.J. Pretorius, who informed me that, as soon as my sentence was confirmed, I would be ordered to wear military uniform and, should I refuse, my civilian clothes would be forcibly removed. Then he added chillingly, 'In Ireland they are dying of hunger and here they can die of cold. Like Bobby Sands, it's your choice.'

For anyone who has been exposed to a highveld winter his was no idle threat. While the days are mostly sunny, a biting cold wind can cut to the bone. At night temperatures can drop to well below freezing. My cell had bars in place of a window and so it was fully exposed to the elements. As it was, the two blankets I had been issued with were not adequate and I had taken to sleeping fully clothed in order to keep warm. The military were clearly intent on making an example of me in order to deter any other conscripts thinking of refusing military service. It was equally clear that they were taking as their model and justification the actions of the British authorities in the Maze prison. I could bleat that my commitment to non-violence placed me in a different category to the IRA, but I doubted that this would avail much.

Contemplating my situation, I resolved that attack is the best form of defence. When the Commanding Officer of the

Detention Barracks, Major Krige, summoned me to show me the notice confirming my sentence, I said as firmly as I could that I would charge him with assault if he ordered my clothes to be forcibly removed. It was a long shot because I had very little confidence that the law would provide a prisoner in detention barracks with any protection, especially when it would be a simple matter to label me as unpatriotic and as a troublemaker. Nevertheless, I realised that I had nothing to lose and hoped that the Director of Military Law had over-played his hand by linking my refusal to wear military uniform with the actions of the IRA hunger strikers. His remark, coming so soon after the death of Bobby Sands, was, at the very least callous and a judge might find it offensive. Moreover, while there were some similarities between my situation and that of the IRA in the Maze prison, there was also a world of a difference.

I think Major Krige thought I was bluffing because he took little notice. He ordered me back to my cell and gave instructions for me to be issued with the military uniform. The uniform was duly delivered to my cell by a corporal, who conveyed an order from Major Krige that I should change out of my civilian clothes, put on the military uniform and be ready for inspection in half an hour. The time passed quickly enough. Major Krige then appeared with a posse of other warders come to witness the fun. Then all became slow motion. They all stood outside the barred door of my cell leering at me inside. Some at the back of the group stood on tiptoe, craning their heads to get a better view of what I was about to do. Major Krige then personally ordered me to hand over my civilian clothes and to put on military uniform.

I said and did nothing. I doubt whether it was possible for me to speak anyway, because my throat became inordinately dry, the blood was pounding in my head, and all my senses were straining to find a means of escape. But there was no escape, save for the total humiliation of giving in. This was my high noon. Major Krige then sent for a straitjacket. When this was brought, he gave me an ultimatum: 'Yeats,' he said, 'remove your civilian clothes and put on the uniform or else I shall unlock this door and we shall remove your clothes for you. If you resist, we will place you in this straitjacket.' At the sight of the forbidding contraption, and having heard of prisoners being suffocated in them, I panicked and undressed in as dignified a manner as I could. I then handed the clothes through the bars of the door and asked to see a lawyer.

My request for a lawyer was ignored while all crowded around to get a view of me and to witness the next part of the game. Major Krige, gloating in triumph at having prized my civilian clothes off me, now reminded me that he had also ordered me to put on the military uniform. Thinking that they were going to burst into the cell at any moment in order to place the straitjacket on me, I had by this stage moved to the back of the cell. He said he would repeat the order and did so. Now more afraid of the humiliation of surrendering where Peter and Richard had stood firm, I summoned up all my draining reserves of courage and managed to whisper that I had refused military service and therefore must refuse to wear military uniform. 'Fine,' he said, thoroughly enjoying himself, 'we'll just leave you then to think things over.'

The lawyer I requested was not summoned for several days. My sole means of keeping warm were two blankets. They were removed in the morning and handed back to me at night. I spent most of the time in my breezy cell, with its slopping out bucket and a mattress on the floor. With no company and nothing to read, there was plenty of time to think about the cold. I took to pacing up and down the cell in order to keep my circulation going. My cell door was opened for mealtimes and I was told that, if I wanted to eat, I would have to join the other prisoners in the open-air mess yard. This presented me with the choice of effectively going on hunger strike in my cell or of making a spectacle of myself in the pair of boxer shorts I had been issued with in order to go outside. The decision was made for me by the cold. Thanking the years I had spent at boarding school for its regime of public cold showers, I joined the long queue of prisoners collecting their food and sat down at a table especially reserved for me. It was one of those moments when one wished for a perfect physique.

Interestingly, none of my fellow inmates ever poked fun at the blue cold wretch who joined them at mealtimes. I think had they done so I would have found it almost unbearable. I like to think that they had a sneaking regard for what I was doing and would have liked to join me. Most of them were young men who simply had had enough of life in the army or had got into scrapes back home, and then had gone absent without leave (AWOL). There were supposed to be a few hardened criminals and psychopathic killers among them, who were considered too violent even for use by Koevoet. They had to be put away somewhere. They were spoken about in hushed whispers by prisoners and warders alike and were given a very wide berth. I remember being puzzled by how immature some of them looked and wondered if it was really true that they had become the merciless killers they were rumoured to be.

By the time a lawyer was called to see me, I had been without clothes for some days and was hyperventilating. The inability to control the pace of my breathing was unnerving and I was beginning to wonder how long I could last. Fortunately, Major Krige decided that I could not be seen in such a state and arranged for me to be examined by the prison doctor. The doctor concluded that the only thing wrong with me was that I urgently needed to be clothed and, in an unexpected display of professional independence, he wrote a note insisting that I be provided with adequate clothing. Major Krige was forced to relent and supplied me with a pair of blue overalls used for work in the prison gardens. I was more than content to put them on as they were similar to the overalls worn by my parents' gardener and sported no military insignia. They were also made of a sufficiently sturdy material to keep out the wind and to keep me tolerably warm.

When he was finally admitted, my lawyer was still

sufficiently concerned about me to rush through an application to the Pretoria Supreme Court for the return of my civilian clothing. The action he brought before the Supreme Court was certainly ambitious. It charged with assault Major Krige; the Chief of the Defence Force, General Constand Viljoen; and the Minister of Defence, General Magnus Malan. In naming the last two senior figures, I feared we had overplayed our hand. But to my relief, Judge Gordon of the Supreme Court did not dismiss the case out of hand and deferred judgement.

Although I was prevented from attending, and therefore am unable to give a personal account of the hearing, the judge appears to have had some sympathy for my situation because he rejected allegations submitted by the prison censor that sought to portray me as perverse. These allegations were based on sentences in letters that had been intercepted by the prison censor and which were held to have 'sinister connotations'. Judge Gordon even went so far as to say that I was clearly not 'a perverse man but someone who is acting out of deeply held beliefs' and that he was therefore prepared to deal with the matter more leniently than he would have in the case of someone who was wilfully perverse. In the resulting state of limbo, when the military were not sure whether the removal of my civilian clothes amounted to an assault, it was decided that I was best left wearing the blue overalls. I had won a reprieve, at least for the time being.

Another reason for the backdown by the DB authorities was that, unbeknown to me, my case was receiving widespread publicity in the media. The two archbishops at my trial had ignited interest in the case. My trial also coincided with an investigation into atrocities allegedly committed by Koevoet on the Namibian border by a delegation set up by the Southern African Catholic Bishops' Conference. The fact that I was not some 'hairy lefty' but a very ordinary young rugby playing South African may have helped. Then the report my solicitor gave of my clothes being removed under threat of force, which included the callous remark about the IRA hunger striker

Bobby Sands, gave my story some momentum. Suddenly, I was something of a hero – at least to sympathisers in the liberal South African press and to some South African parents, who bitterly resented the dangers and privations imposed on their sons in the border war in Namibia and in the South African townships.

The real hero of the moment, however, was a United Reformed Minister, Rob Robertson. He was the Convener of the Commission on Violence and Non-Violence of the South African Council of Churches. He was at the same time the minister of St Antony's, a United Presbyterian and Congregational church in the poor neighbourhood of Pageview, Johannesburg. Rob and Gert, his wife, were tireless peace activists, deeply committed to the practice of non-violence or, as Gandhi called it, *satyagraha*. Thanks to him there was a network throughout South Africa of journalists, human rights lawyers and church workers ready to support young people in my predicament. Behind his mild mannered exterior, he was probably more subversive of the South African regime than anyone will give him credit for.

Rob acquired a copy of the statement read out by the president of my court martial and subjected it to a searching critique in several papers. He made the following observations:

1. Is it not religious persecution if a court recognises the honesty of an opinion based on a Christian attitude and then goes on to impose a sentence as a '*corrective*' measure and in order to 'discourage similar attitudes'?
2. It is true and tragic that young national servicemen give their lives or are maimed. The responsibility lies with the older generation who voted in the government and not with the young conscientious objector who opposes war.
3. The 'ivory tower' in which Charles Yeats 'may be living' was actually the Diocesan Office in Windhoek from which he travelled unarmed, in unarmoured vehicles, to churches in remote parts of the operational area.

He concluded that the law was in need of revision in order to avoid the kind of muddle my court martial had got itself into and in order to provide the kind of non-military form of national service that I had proposed and which would help address the root causes of conflict in South African society.

In addition to an endless series of press reports and comment on my situation in DB, Rob used his role in the SACC to ensure that I was not forgotten by the churches. He prepared a statement supporting my stand from the heads or prospective heads of all the mainline denominations, which was distributed to the major newspapers. The signatories were Mr Chris Aitken, General Secretary, Presbyterian Church of Southern Africa; The Rt Rev François Bill, Moderator, Tsonga Presbyterian Church; The Most Rev Bill Burnett, Archbishop of Cape Town, Church of the Province of Southern Africa; Rev Dr John de Gruchy, Chairman, United Congregational Church of Southern Africa, The Most Rev Denis Hurley, President, Southern African Catholic Bishops' Conference; The Rev Howard Kirkby, President, Methodist Conference of Southern Africa, The Rev Stanley Magoba, Secretary designate, Methodist Church of Southern Africa; Rt Rev Philip Russell, Bishop of Natal, Archbishop elect of Cape Town; and The Rt Rev Brian Woods, Moderator, General Assembly, Presbyterian Church of Southern Africa. With the glaring absences of the leaders of the Dutch Reformed Churches, it was a pretty united stance. The concluding paragraph of the statement reads as follows:

> We urge the Government to understand that, in the present circumstances of our country, conscientious objection to military service can be based on genuine religious and moral belief. We urge the Government at the earliest possible opportunity to regularise the position of conscientious objectors through the provision of alternative non-military forms of national service, and in the mean time to exercise in regard to Charles Yeats, and all other conscientious objectors, the humanity that should be characteristic of a Christian society.

Even before my trial, Rob had contacted Amnesty International, the human rights organisation based in London, which adopted me as a prisoner of conscience. This had one very important practical effect. By the second week of my detention, letters of support from members of Amnesty were literally pouring in from all over the world. The letters gave the impression that DB was under an international spotlight. Major Krige and his fellow officers, many of whom would never have travelled abroad, could not but sit up and take notice, especially when the envelopes arrived bearing stamps from faraway places.

At first all the letters were handed over to me. They greatly helped buoy my spirits and I cannot express enough of my amazement and gratitude that people from distant continents, such as India and Asia, which I have never even visited, took the time to write. The concern of two people, in particular, was so impressive that I must single them out. Masami Kojima, a Japanese engineer, living in the United States, who had never met me and was unlikely ever to do so, wrote every week of my sentence. Another who wrote every month was the formidable President of the Black Sash, a women's anti-apartheid organisation in South Africa, Sheena Duncan. She was a revered figure in the English-speaking community for her courage and sense of humour and always conjured up for me the slogan of the march of the women on Pretoria: 'When you strike the women, you have struck a rock.' I loved receiving Sheena's letters and picturing Major Krige reading them before me and quaking. All who wrote ensured that I was not forgotten.

The letters, media publicity and the Supreme Court's reserved judgement joined to calm the atmosphere in DB that I had ruffled by refusing the order to wear military uniform. In the circumstances, there was very little the military could do to me. I was left in the blue overalls and assigned a portion of the garden to tend. Left to myself, I was the model prisoner, who willingly responded to all reasonable requests and who had no plan to escape. After a while, lazy warders did not even bother to lock me up at night. I exercised my right to study and enrolled in a theology degree with UNISA, South Africa's Open University. As long as I kept my head down, the days passed pleasantly enough.

Keeping one's head down, though, was more difficult to do than one might think, because it proved virtually impossible to ignore the violence that was a daily occurrence in DB. The sole purpose of this institution was to deliver a sufficiently 'short, sharp shock' to deter further wrongdoing on the front line, where the army wanted each soldier to be. There was no attempt to rehabilitate inmates or to assist with their social problems, such as getting a girl into trouble, which was the most common reason for their going AWOL. DB, therefore, was a purely penal institution and dealt out a daily dose of systematic brutality, which I could not help observing from the sidelines. Each day the abuse of fellow human beings faced me with the question, 'Why am I not doing something about the violence? What sort of a human being am I, that I can crawl away into my little foxhole and leave others to be brutally treated?' This question began to gnaw away at me as I reflected on the inconsistency that I had sought to oppose the violence outside DB but was doing nothing about the violence within.

The question became increasingly focused for me in relation to one particular individual. He was a young corporal, who, by virtue of his junior rank, was often on night duty, when the absence of senior officers gave him and the other junior warders free run of the prison. One night he received a squad of new inmates transferred from another prison and began to show them who was boss by drilling them in an open space not far from my cell. I could hear every blow struck, and could feel their terror seeping through the walls of my cell. I also knew that my cell had not been locked and therefore it was possible for me to intervene if I wanted to. I lay for what seemed a long time unable to make up my mind until, finally, I could bear no more and something snapped within me. I burst out of the cell and halted the punishment by placing myself between the squad and their tormentor. He was of course enraged and had me forcibly removed to the punishment cells until the morning.

A second incident occurred with this same corporal on the parade ground some weeks later. He was abusing and making a public spectacle of a thin, sickly looking conscript, who, lacking co-ordination, found it impossible to march in step. I was working in the nearby garden hoping one of the senior officers present would put a stop to the bullying. When no one intervened, the thought struck me that I was once again allowing the abuse of a fellow human being, without lifting a finger. I realised that the brutality had almost become routine for me and that I was beginning to not even notice. This time though, having cut my teeth in the previous incident, I was less scared. I strode on to the parade ground and insisted the corporal stop. Fortunately for me, my action drew the attention of senior officers, who rushed to restore order and to save me from a possible lynching.

I only recall this incident here because, with many of my fellow White South Africans, we must continue to live with the shame that there were so many such actions we should have taken but did not. We simply failed to act. We sat on the 'Whites Only' seats, used the 'Whites Only' toilets, swam off the 'Whites Only' beaches, attended the 'Whites Only' schools, and lived in the 'Whites Only' areas. We failed to act when we knew that human beings of the calibre of Nelson Mandela were sitting year after year numbingly breaking rocks in our jails. We failed to act when we heard accounts of torture and death in detention, such as that of Steve Biko, the charismatic leader of the Black Consciousness Movement. We failed to act when whole communities of mainly old men, women and children were uprooted from their homes and dumped in barren Bantu homelands. We failed to act when the mines took the men away from their wives and families and housed them in single sex hostels, calling down the holocaust of AIDS.

We simply failed to act. We looked away. We played sport.

And I played a lot of sport. Like those early settlers, who marked the massacres of their families and friends in the Natal Drakensberg at the hands of Dingane's Zulu impis by naming a town *Weenen* (weeping), we, the White survivors of apartheid, can never think of South Africa without pain. Now and forever there will always be a part of us that weeps.

8

PRISON VISITS

A BaSotho blanket is colourful and warm. It must be heavy because the BaSotho live in the cold Maluti Mountains. The village of Teyateyaneng straddles one of the foothills and our home had a view of the mountains.

('BaSotho Blanket', Christmas 1981)

One Sunday a month I was allowed a visit. According to prison rules, visits were restricted to immediate members of one's family. A fiancée counted as family. As my parents could not make the long journey across South Africa from Durban and I was not married, Rob Robertson chose for me René Rademan, an attractive young woman with raven-black hair, from among the unattached members of his congregation to act as my fiancée. She braved the vast military complex of Voortrekkerhoogte each month to sit with me for two hours and bring me my UNISA course work and news of the outside world.

Visits were policed by an elderly warder, Staff Sergeant Jooste. Staaff, as he was affectionately known by all, was an Afrikaner who could barely speak a word of English. He would turn up on Sundays without fail and relish the responsibility of personally vetting each of the visitors and letting them know that their visit was entirely at his discretion.

He would greet each one at the outer gate of DB, conduct a body search if he suspected there were any concealed drugs, cigarettes, or perhaps a weapon, and then escort the visitor the fifty metres to the inner gate, where he would hand them over to another warder and the awaiting prisoner. The prisoner and his visitor would then sit together at a table with a guard sitting nearby and in earshot.

Rob Robertson's arrangement worked very well and I hugely looked forward to my visits from René. However, like all devious schemes it came unstuck. Some six months after I had started my sentence, I received a letter from Alison to inform me that she had started her elective at Bethesda and would be visiting me the following month. But I knew that this would not be possible because Staaff could not miss the Titian hair. He had personally vetted both my parents and, on several occasions, my raven-haired 'fiancée'. The worst part was that I could not think of a way of getting a message out to warn her that the long journey from northern Zululand to DB was hopeless. There was therefore nothing to do but wait in abject misery.

Eventually the ghastly day arrived. Desperately hoping at least for a glimpse of her, I positioned myself at the inner gate, beyond which prisoners were not permitted to go, and waited. The wait seemed endless. Then I saw her. Alison and Staaff were locked in conversation, which I knew to be mutually incomprehensible because Alison knew no Afrikaans and Staaff so little English that it did not count. But Alison was not giving up and Staaff was not giving in. My misery deepened. I decided to wave to catch her attention. She looked up and waved back, which had Staaff look round and see me. Curious as to know who this very foreign English woman was, he then ordered her to stay put while he walked over to question me.

But Staaff had underestimated Alison. She left her post and walked over to the inner gate, reaching it just as he opened it and asked me who the devil this woman was who was so insistent on visiting me. There then followed one of the most momentous exchanges of my life. I said to Staaff in Afrikaans, knowing that Alison would not understand, 'Die is die meisie met wie ek will trou.' (This is the girl I am going to marry.) He replied, 'Nee, Yeats, dis nie jou meisie nie. Ek weet jou meisie het swart hare.' (No, Yeats, this is not your fiancée. I know your girl has black hair.) No amount of entreaty would budge him. 'Asseblief', (Please) I pleaded, 'Sy kom van Engeland af om my te sien.' (She has come from England to see me.)

With no sign from Staaff that he was prepared to budge, I turned to Alison and proposed to her on the spot. 'Will you be my wife?' I said, loud and clear. Staaff appeared to understand that something significant was taking place; perhaps, he had seen a man propose before at the cinema, or, if he had a wife, was able to recall the moment he had proposed. Whatever the reason, he read the body language and turned to look intently at Alison. We both waited expectantly for her response.

Alison has often let me down, but never quite as badly as she did at the inner gate of the detention barracks at Voortrekkerhoogte. She kept her composure and replied, 'I need to think about it.' After all the encouragement she had given me since our first encounter at St Helens, Bishopsgate, it was not the response I was expecting. I was devastated. Staaff immediately sensed from my crestfallen look that I had been disappointed and seized on this with glee. 'Ja, Yeats' (Yes, Yeats), he shouted, 'jy sien, dis *nie* jou meisie nie.' (You see, she is *not* your girl.) 'Jy jok met my net.' (You are just joking with me.) He then took Alison firmly by the elbow and ushered her back to the outer gate. I was by now so thoroughly crushed and humiliated, that I slunk away back to my cell, never wanting to see Alison ever again.

Once again Staaff underestimated Alison. Whether it was her persistence or a demonic sense of humour on his part, we will never know, but he relented and allowed the visit after all. I was summoned from my cell and spent one of the most uncomfortable two hours of my life talking to a girl who, in a moment of tension and feeling, I had proposed to and who, to top it all, had turned me down. I recall that our conversation was so stilted that even the guard sent into the room with us soon lost interest. I could not get the visit over with more quickly.

One visit I never wanted to end was when all the members of my family visited me on Christmas Day. None of them had ever set foot inside a prison. The face of my youngest brother, Gavin, was the most expressive. Still then a schoolboy, one could see that he had entered in his imagination a dungeon so foul and so cruel, that he expected to see me chained to the wall. My younger brother, Michael, was even quieter than usual. Of the two of us he has always been the more sensible and discreetly avoided military service by joining the police force for a year. I could hear him silently saying to himself, 'Well, Charles, you have really got yourself into it now.' My dear parents wore a look of suffering bewilderment, which comes from having a child, whom you have spent a lifetime keeping from danger, placed beyond a parent's protection. Only my grandmother was up to the occasion. True to form and entirely unruffled, she had Staff Sergeant Jooste scurrying about providing seating for her entire family.

In anticipation of their visit, I had prepared for them a gift. It was a short vignette of our family's life in Basutoland. I gave my account the title 'BaSotho Blanket', on account of the way our lives there had been colourful and warm, like the blankets worn by the BaSotho people. I hoped it would help transport us on Christmas Day out of the dingy room in DB and apartheid South Africa to the little English village of Teyateyaneng, of which we all had happy memories – especially of Christmas, when the whole Yeats clan in Basutoland and South Africa gathered together at the local hotel, the Blue Mountain Inn, for dinner on Christmas Eve.

Christmas Day started with a service at the Club, followed by drinks and lunch at my grandparents' home, the Top House. There we were joined by the other village trading family, the Tullys. The cold lunch included turkey, ham, mock venison (mutton dressed up in spices and bacon), braun (a mélange of meats), new potatoes and salad, followed by homemade ice cream and watermelon. When the adults had worked through their champagne and food, we got down to what, for us children, was the serious part of the day, brush cricket. This game was played according to rules developed to limit the damage to the flowerbeds and to take account of the peculiar topography of the garden and its buildings; you were out, for instance, if caught off one thatched roof but scored a six if you landed on another roof. It also had special rules for individual members of the family, such as my grandmother's stepbrother, Ian Dare, a Billy Bunter-type character with an artificial leg, who took the leg off and knelt to bat and then, when given out, roaring his protest at the umpire's decision, would hop to the swimming pool and dive in with a crash. Every Christmas at Teyateyaneng was a day to remember.

I tried to evoke special memories for each of my guests by recalling different aspects of their lives. Starting with the great matriarch present, I recalled the Top House, with its rambling collection of thatched rondavels, which she and my grandfather made the centre of the British Empire. Anyone of any consequence in Basutoland would have enjoyed her gracious hospitality served on the best Royal Worcester china. They would also have listened to my scholarly grandfather's tales of cannibals, gun-running and the wisdom of the first king of the BaSotho, Moshoeshwe, who provided a refuge in the Maluti Mountains during the *Mfecane* (The Crushing) for Bantu fleeing warlords, such as Shaka. He was a fund of these stories, having been brought up at the foot of Moshoeshwe's natural mountain fortress of Thaba Bosiu, where my great-grandfather John Yeats, himself a Scottish refugee from the weather and poverty of Paisley near Glasgow, established the first Yeats trading post in 1881. My grandfather had followed by setting up his first mountain trading post at Thaba Bosigo in 1911, and then had moved to base his business in Teyateyaneng in 1935.

I recalled bowls on the village bowling green my grandfather made the equal of any in England, and how, seventeen years her senior and fiercely competitive, he always used to choose for himself the stronger side. We all laughed (guiltily) at the memory of my grandmother's battle with the 'mad monk' of the Society of the Sacred Mission, who tried to assert his independence and his Christian ideals by moving the convenient Sunday service for Whites held at the Club to the mission on the outskirts of the village, where he wanted the whole Christian family to worship together. His mistake was not to change the venue but to move it to a time that clashed with bowls. I also reminded her of her wonderful old cook, Me Diesetso, and her friend Ntunsi, the health worker she helped educate in the United States and who later became a Minister of Health in the Lesotho cabinet.

For my brothers, I recalled our early morning visits to the Top House. We would get into the double bed with my grandfather and watch my grandmother bustling about with rapt fascination. We would keenly watch the ash on the cigarette she always smoked grow longer and longer and longer, until it finally fell off on to her ample bosom and provoked a howl of abuse. Getting to know her better when I was older, I suspect that she did it to entertain us. She brought joy to all in a no-nonsense down-to-earth way. We all adored her and, on her birthday, vied with each other to make speeches in her honour. Her double bed was also a safe refuge from our parents' wrath.

I recalled Wesi and Thabo, the two BaSotho friends from whom we were inseparable and who shared in all the activities little boys get up to. They were our only companions because there were no other White children in the village. I reminded them of the pathetically small amounts of pocket money my father gave us on Saturdays and how we always found a better deal at the store of the other trading family in Teyateyaneng, the Tullys. We would buy our sweets and tins of condensed milk and then climb on to the tall stack of BaSotho blankets above my father's office for the feast. When we were not playing tennis or swimming we would saddle up our BaSotho ponies, Thokolosi and Ginger, and ride through the unfenced countryside without a care in the world.

For my parents, I described their first married home, with its wide arc of floor-to-ceiling windows in the living room overlooking the majestic blue Maluti Mountains. Their evenings together would start with the magic hour, twilight, that lingering, warm hour in Africa when the light gradually fades and the stars come out. This is when, with whisky and soda in hand, the expatriate Englishman counts himself the most fortunate and relaxed person in the world. With their small army of servants, year-round sunshine, large garden with its peach, pear and mulberry trees, and swimming pool, their quality of life was better than that of any English aristocrat.

My father lived for his polo, and so I recalled the Yeats polo team, consisting of my father (the provincial captain), my Uncle Gerald (a junior Springbok), and their two cousins, Murray and Neal. The last two were less skilful but played with a recklessness that unnerved the most steely opponents. I also listed each of his favourite polo ponies, Achieve, Jesamba, Corbett and Mainstreet, and extolled their respective virtues and vices on and off the polo field. I knew each one intimately because most mornings of my school holidays would start with a ride to exercise the ponies and to school a novice. Sadly, one morning my father's horse reared and fell back on him, crushing ribs and dislocating a shoulder, leaving me, age six, to ride back to camp alone for help. He somehow managed to drag himself to the road where we laid him in the back of a lorry and rushed him to the nearest hospital. Although he recovered, he never played polo to the same standard again, which ended the round of polo tournaments that took us as a family all over Southern Africa.

My father also impressively built up something of a Basutoland trading empire. In addition to three stores and a wholesale business in Teyateyaneng, Yeats and Dare Pty Ltd came to own the trading stations of Nene's, Matekas, Peka, Pitseng, Qalaheng, Leribe, Kolonyama, Mamathes, Berea Hills and Ramokilane. I recalled how my brothers and I would perch dangerously on the back of four-wheel-drive trucks carrying merchandise to many of these remote mountain outposts. Once there we would find a way into the large sheds stacked with bales of wool and mohair, which the BaSotho traded for the staple supplies sold in the store. We would play hide and seek, emerging black with dirt. On the way back, we would stop at one of the mountain streams for a swim and to clean up before our mother saw us.

For my mother, I recalled her impressive exploits as a tennis player, which included selection as a Wimbledon hopeful. Village life was not always easy for her. Her energetic and forceful mother-in-law could not refrain from being the dominant personality in the village and, in such a small community, could not help intruding on her son's marriage from time to time. My grandmother was also an impossible act to follow. Beyond gardening, entertaining the occasional guest, there was not a great deal to do when all household chores were taken care of by servants and women were not expected to work. My mother's great sadness was that her first child and only daughter, Cheryl Ann, was stillborn. The BaSotho gave me the name TsiLiso, which means compensation, because I was the next to be born. But her three sons could never quite make up for the loss of a daughter and companion. After teaching each of us for our first year of school and then sending us off to boarding school, she set up a Red Cross postnatal clinic in the village.

For all our amusement, I recalled some of the stories of Roger Tully, for many years the delinquent bachelor of Teyateyaneng. He was forever trying to lead my father and uncle and then my brothers and me astray, until he was finally tamed by marriage to his long-suffering girlfriend, Mabel. He was largely responsible for my first and only hangover, which followed a New Year's Eve party at the Blue Mountain Inn, and which ended in my grandparents' double bed the next morning with my grandmother plying me with cups and cups of tea. Roger had a similar character in Jasper, my uncle's dog, who found life too tame at home and who used to roam the village, invariably ending up at the village pub, where he would be offered a drink, lap it up and then weave his way home.

While I tried to tell my story of Basutoland – 'BaSotho Blanket' – with as light a touch as possible, it stirred up strong emotions in my audience because some part of us all mourned Teyateyaneng. Our misfortune as a family was to have lived at the end of the colonial era, which had taken our forebears out from Britain and gave them to think that the British enclaves they created for themselves in Africa were permanent. This was a cruel illusion, which was shattered in Harold Macmillan's famous 'Winds of Change' speech of 1961, when he gave notice that Britain would be withdrawing from its African colonies. Such was the lack of preparation for independence in Basutoland that, as happened in many former African colonies, Westminster-style democracy lasted no longer than the first parliament. After losing the popular vote in 1970, the defeated Prime Minister Lebua Jonathan dissolved parliament and proceeded to rule as a dictator. A low intensity civil war followed. With the prospect of a worsening political and economic situation, our whole extended family was eventually forced to leave Lesotho for neighbouring South Africa, with its much larger White population.

My grandmother wiped back some tears and then gruffly handed over her Christmas present to me. It was the hamper she used to pack for boarding school: homemade fruitcake and biscuits, dried fruit, biltong and bars of chocolate. Staff Sergeant Jooste had attempted to confiscate the lot but she had fended him off by reminding him that it was Christmas Day and by saying that she could see from the look of him that he was a good Christian. I tucked into this Babette's feast with relish after they had left, as I had already lost a stone on prison rations.

Alison was able to fit in one more visit to DB during her three-month medical elective in Zululand. This time, Staaff let her in without demur. Before retreating to deal with other visitors, he provided a chair for her and, behind her back, raised his eyebrows at me. The craggy old fellow even managed a wink. I found this encouragement unhelpful, given the awkward note on which our previous visit ended and my month long misery for having proposed so intemperately to Alison. She must have noticed my discomfort because she immediately broke into a hair-raising report of her time at Bethesda mission hospital.

The flying doctor service had taken her on flights all over northern Zululand and right up to the border with Mozambique. She was most animated about an excursion to the wilderness of Kosi Bay, just south of the Mozambique border. This angler's paradise is one of the largest freshwater lakes in southern Africa. At the time it was deserted, save for the most intrepid fishermen, on account of the civil war raging in Mozambique, which tended to spill over the porous border. The pilot landed by the lake and encouraged Alison and another Bart's medical student, serving her elective at the nearby Manguzi mission hospital, to take a swim. The two young women had not thought to bring their costumes, so they walked to a secluded cove and, as only two Englishwomen would in Africa, in the middle of nowhere, bathed in their underwear. In all their innocence, what they never realised was that they swam in waters teeming with hippos and that the hippo kills more humans than any other wild animal in Africa.

The danger they had unwittingly exposed themselves to did not stop there. On returning to the plane, a puncture in one of the two tyres was discovered when they were taxiing on to the makeshift runway. This caused the plane to go round in circles. The pilot attempted several remedies, including stuffing the flat tyre with grass and, when this did not work, he replaced the grass with spare clothing left in the plane. I wondered to myself how he had justified to himself the risk of taking off and then landing with his two precious passengers on one good wheel. Mercifully, the clothes did not work either. They were then stranded, miles and miles from anywhere until a passing fishing boat rescued them.

To my horror, for no White South African ever risked it, Alison went on to report that she had hitchhiked into neighbouring Swaziland. When I responded that I had never hitchhiked in Africa, she assured me that she had not gone alone and that she and her companion, another English girl, had refused a lift from two truckers. Her guardian angel must have intervened because, soon after the trucks drove on, they were offered a lift by an expatriate couple working in Swaziland. The couple, who had daughters themselves, were so concerned to come across two English girls on a deserted stretch of African road that they insisted on driving the girls to Swaziland and then back to Bethesda after their weekend jaunt. She rounded off this tale of narrow escapes with an encounter she had with a green mamba, the most poisonous snake in Africa, which she had nearly put a hand on as it lay draped across the garden gate of her lodgings.

Alison concluded with an account of her work. She could not get over the difference between the sanitised medicine practised in the NHS and the raw medicine at Bethesda, where the few indispensable doctors dealt with any emergency and did what they could as best they could. She said that she had learned to deal with a cholera outbreak, with only the scantiest medical supplies and equipment. She had participated in some incredible feats of surgery and had treated a wide variety of injuries, such as an axe still embedded in the head of a woman victim of domestic violence. One evening she anxiously listened while the Medical Director talked through a procedure on a two-way radio to an inexperienced doctor at a nearby hospital. The surgery involved drilling a burr hole to release a blood clot in a patient's brain; the conversation ended abruptly when the patient died.

At the time of her elective, the mission hospital was in the process of being handed over to the KwaZulu homeland medical health service. The transition was not a happy one. The new, inadequately trained medical administrators were so inept that in the cholera outbreak they ordered plasma tubes but not the stands on which to place the bottles of plasma. The improvised solution to the crisis was to have teams of nurses holding the bottles aloft. Many of the nurses lacked the dedicated nursing values taken so much for granted in the NHS. As a result wards were left dirty and patients were often ill-treated. Some of the doctors were no better. Worst of all were the White medical students from Johannesburg, who spent short periods at Bethesda gaining experience of rural medicine. They appeared in fleets of expensive Mercedes Benz motorcars, contemptuously ordered the Black medical staff about and displayed appalling medical ignorance. Alison's encounters left her with no illusions about the new medical service and she wistfully recalled the visit we made together when the hospital was still under the control of selfless, South African medical missionaries.

Bethesda had clearly been an eye-opening experience, one that had put Western medicine in context. But it had also been a huge adventure. The telling took up most of our two hours together, leaving no time for addressing the subject that was uppermost in both our minds. However, when she rose to leave, she held out a hand with a simple ring on her wedding finger that I had not noticed. She said she had thought about my offer and, after careful consideration, decided to accept me. The ring was for me to put on if I still wanted to.

9

SOLITARY CONFINEMENT

Lord, whatever this day may bring,
Thy name be praised.

(Dietrich Bonhoeffer, *Prayers for Fellow Prisoners*)

After the death of Bobby Sands, a further nine hunger strikers in the Maze Prison were allowed to die. They were aged between twenty-five and twenty-seven. More would have died were it not for the intervention of some of the mothers who agreed to sign the form permitting the prison authorities to begin feeding their sons once they had fallen into a coma and were no longer able to take responsibility for themselves. Their actions effectively ended the hunger strike. Considering the history of English colonisation of Ireland and of Protestant persecution of Catholics in Northern Ireland, while the IRA may have been misguided in resorting to violence, what cannot be denied is that these young men were victims of a terrible historical injustice. They deserved better than Margaret Thatcher.

Without access to newspapers in DB, I was oblivious of this drama. I had assumed that the strike had ended when Bobby Sands died the week before my trial. I was therefore unaware that other prisoners had joined the strike and were dying in the Maze Prison in the months I was awaiting judgement in the case of assault I had brought against the SADF for forcibly removing my clothes. While they suffered their slow death of dehydration and starvation, I peacefully went about the prison garden, cutting the grass borders and watering the vygies, a hardy little plant with tiny, brightly coloured flowers. When no one was looking, I would find a patch of shade and pull out one of the small cards from the memory pack of Bible verses an evangelical friend had given me, with the advice that learning them off by heart would be a good use of any spare time.

My pair of blue overalls, my only item of clothing, had worn very soft and the colour had faded in the sun to a fashionable denim. They had become such old friends that I wondered why people choose to wear other types of clothing when overalls are so comfortable, serviceable and warm. They also represented for me the small victory I had won over the mighty SADF. I could not help walking past Major Krige and thinking to my quiet satisfaction that the sight of me in blue overalls was a thorn in his side. The Supreme Court Judge was taking so long in delivering his judgement that it looked as if he might delay until my sentence was over. I dreamt of handing back Major Krige his blue overalls, solemnly bowing to him, and then walking naked and free out of the prison gates, like Francis of Assisi.

But this triumphant end to my time in DB was not to be. Judge Gordon finally gave his judgement against me in August. Essentially he ruled that the Detention Barrack authorities were entitled to require me to wear military uniform. Major Krige and his henchmen outside my cell with their straitjacket were therefore exonerated. There was one glimmer of hope though for me. The judgement left undecided the crucial issue of whether, had the Detention Barrack authorities physically removed my clothes, this would have constituted assault. Fortunately, Major Krige chose not to test this possibility because, this time, I was determined not to panic, and planned to lie in a foetal position on my bed and force them to rip my friendly overall off me. However, the

Director of Military Law, who had threatened me with the fate of Bobby Sands, was not happy to let me get off too lightly. He had to live up to Margaret Thatcher, and set about enforcing to the limit what he could legally do to me in DB with full vigour.

The day after the judgement, Major Krige summoned me from working in the prison garden to his office. He explained that my legal status was of a soldier under his command and, therefore, should I refuse a lawful command he could impose a maximum sentence of fourteen days of solitary confinement in the punishment cells. The rules allowed one day of grace before he could repeat the punishment. He insisted that he was prepared to indefinitely repeat the punishment. Furthermore, he pointed out that, once my sentence was completed, there was nothing preventing the SADF calling me up again and again and again until I was sixty-five.

My prospects had suddenly changed. I found myself sitting in a small cell for twenty-three out of twenty-four hours of the day (one hour for ablutions and exercise) for fourteen days at a stretch. With no reading matter or writing materials, confinement in such a small space requires a measure of self-control. It also demands a certain inventiveness if one is not to climb up the wall and stand upside down on the ceiling. I coped in three basic ways.

Firstly, I took regular bouts of exercise in the cell and vigorous exercise in the hour outside. There was a small patch of grass between the punishment cells and the main prison block, which I used to jog and sprint around in a figure of eight for as long as I was allowed. While jogging, I relived my school runs to Otto's Bluff overlooking the Umgeni Valley, the run through sugar-cane fields to the wonderful views over the Indian ocean above Umhlanga Rocks and, my favourite run of all, on the famous Robberg beach, part of the seaside resort of Plettenberg Bay, in the eastern Cape. Sinking into the rhythm of my body, I would remember the packed sand at low tide, the sunset colouring the water and my feet following the jagged foam line. In this way I experienced something of the wonderful sense of freedom and wellbeing that one has running in the sunshine, with the wind and the spray of the surf in one's hair.

In my cell, I practised a variation of the Canadian exercises my father had taught me. These included the usual stretches, push-ups, back arches and then sit-ups. I did these at intervals during the day. They were especially important last thing at night, when they helped me sleep. Going through my routine was always pleasing, as I was able to picture my dad doing his daily round of exercises in his underpants and looking more monkey than man with his great hairy chest. He had passed on the daily discipline of these exercises to each of his sons by inviting us to perform them with him from an early age. Although they get more difficult to do as one gets older, and the expanding waistline of one of my brothers shows signs that he has abandoned them, they remain one of my dad's lasting legacies to us.

Secondly, I used to pray. It is difficult to describe my deepening experience of prayer without risking merely repeating what the many mystics of the past have written, but two facets of the experience stand out.

One was an overwhelming physical sense of a kindly presence. On occasions I felt a strange warm, tingling sensation, spreading from my head down to my hands and then feet. I had experienced this before fleetingly in prayer. The difference in my cell was that the experience was more prolonged. I will of course never know for certain whether what I experienced was merely a physical and psychological reaction to the extreme pressures of my situation. But having had the experience before at different times when I was not under any particular pressure, I welcomed what I believe to be a mysterious existence outside of myself making itself known to me. My companion made solitary confinement no longer solitary. Indeed, even now there is a part of me that will ever be the hermit wanting to return to the punishment cells of DB, and I content myself with the thought that life must eventually empty itself of all its business and busyness, leaving space to extend more of an invitation to this very special guest.

The other was the discovery of an inner prompting or voice. Inside prison there was no one to turn to for advice on how to respond to the complex situations that faced me. I came to trust this guide to provide me with essential discernment about what was to be done. Once again I concede that I shall never know for certain whether this experience relates to a mystery beyond the complexity of the human person or whether it is merely the prompting of some innate sixth sense or survival instinct. However, ignoring or denying the prompting of this voice as irrational has invariably turned out to be a mistake. Ever since, faced with all kinds of difficult decisions, I have tried to hear and then obey this inner voice, believing it to be a form of divine guidance.

One final point may be worth making before passing on and that is I do not recall ever feeling downcast in solitary confinement. It was as if I was buoyed up throughout. I would even go so far as to say that I experienced a kind of irrepressible joy. I first became conscious of this after a special visit from the then Anglican Bishop of Pretoria, Michael Nuttall. He enquired very kindly after my mental wellbeing and showed his concern by reading some of the Psalms with me. Perhaps he passed something infectious on to me. Whatever the cause, encumbered as I now am with innumerable worries, responsibilities and material possessions, I cannot help thinking that my experience of joy in what was the most unlikely of places partly came from simply accepting that, stripped of everything, even my freedom, there was nothing else to do but live from day to day. It was an invaluable lesson because the reality of an individual human life is that it is bounded on every side, that none of us is in control of our destiny, and all the honours and possessions we so desperately accumulate to mark ourselves off from others and to underpin our comforts are so terribly disappointing. Whenever I am now downcast, I try to remember this lesson.

My third main way of coping with solitary confinement

was to spend endless hours day-dreaming. As the days went by, I became so practised that I could virtually levitate myself off the bed and take myself off on a flying carpet to wherever I needed to be. In this way, I visited Alison at Bethesda and peered in on her medical rounds. I joined in Peter Baron's Bible study group at St Helen's in London. I sat with Neil and Creena Alcock in their eyrie of a home overlooking the Tugela River. I attended a Diakonia Council meeting, watching Archbishop Hurley diplomatically responding to the concerns of his ecumenical partners. I flew the long, long way to Namibia, where, for a thrill, I sat in the passenger seat of the car being driven by Bishop James on the road to St Mary's, Odibo.

The inefficiencies or 'slack' that plague virtually all human systems also helped soften the impact of solitary confinement. What tended to happen was that for the first few days of a two-week sentence, the twenty-three-hour confinement to a punishment cell was rigidly adhered to. But then there would be a gradual relaxation for all manner of reasons. The main one was that the guard, who supervised my hour outside, much preferred to sit in the sun and doze while I exercised, than perform his other duties. Consequently, my hour spent running would extend to an hour and a half, then to two, and sometimes even to three, if the guard thought he could get away with it. My guard would sometimes be joined by other guards also trying to skive off their duties. When this happened I was always sure to get a long time out because they would happily sun themselves and talk for as long as possible. I simply kept on running and running and running until I was ordered to return to my cell.

In all my time in solitary, there was only one period of serious self-doubt. This was prompted by the appearance of a Cuban pilot, who had been shot down and captured in Angola by South African forces. He was placed in a cell not far from my own. We never spoke and I only got to know about his identity after one of the warders whispered to me in awe that he was a Communist. His presence and my seclusion led me to question whether there was any substance to the accusation made at my court martial that I had underestimated the threat of international Communism and whether, in the light of this threat, a case could be made for military service. As the judge had put it: 'The court has to consider the times in which we live. A military onslaught is being made on our borders and possibly inside them. If those attacking us were only nationalists it would not be so bad. But there is also tremendous pressure from Marxist and non-Christian sources. It is a serious *de facto* situation. Without making too much of it, you have shared your place with strange and dangerous bedmates, people who sin against God.'

After some soul searching, I decided that I probably had underestimated the threat of Communism. Indeed, there was no denying the 'rooi gevaar' as he lived only a few doors down from me. There was also no denying the victorious Marxist-led guerrilla movements in neighbouring Angola and Mozambique. Perhaps I was, after all, terribly misguided and the SADF was protecting South Africa from falling into Communist hands. But would they be worse than White supremacists? The best I could do to dismiss these doubts at the time was to fall back on the support I had received from the three respected witnesses at my trial, Archbishop Hurley, Archbishop Philip Russell and Professor John Dugard. I was pleased when the Cuban was swapped for South African prisoners captured in Angola.

There was plenty of time to try to make sense of a puzzling world because I was sentenced in total to five bouts of solitary confinement. But thanks to Rob Robertson, Major Krige was not having it all his own way. Rob made sure that the papers were fed a regular account of what was happening to his upstanding young man in DB. Dorothy Steele, the mother of the conscientious objector Richard, who had been subjected to several bouts of solitary himself, had decided to campaign against solitary confinement and was exercising all her considerable force of character and charm on Major Krige and the military high command to try to get them to soften their treatment of conscientious objectors. Then the lesson that 'the blood of the martyrs is seed' must slowly have begun to dawn on the military, because, instead of deterring other conscripts, their treatment of me, with all its attendant publicity, was influencing an increasing number to refuse publicly to do military service.

The response of the military to the growing problem I posed was to present me with an ultimatum. At the end of my fifth bout of solitary, Major Krige summoned me and, in the presence of a senior officer, warned that if I again refused his command to wear military uniform, instead of yet another summary trial in DB, he would have me tried by court martial. He there and then commanded me to put on the uniform, perhaps hoping that the shock announcement would bounce me into changing my mind. Fortunately, I did not immediately fully grasp all the implications of what he had said and simply responded to the command in the way I had done before. Thoroughly frustrated, he then yelled at me that he did not want to see me again and ordered that I be taken back to my cell.

To face court martial a second time was unprecedented. Neither Peter Moll nor Richard Steele had been treated in this way. After repeated bouts of solitary confinement, the military had recognised that their spirits were not to be broken and they had been allowed to spend the remainder of their one-year sentence working in the prison garden. What was in store for me?

I had about a month to wait before finding out. Deciding that enough money had been spent on my earlier legal defence and that the outcome was a foregone conclusion anyway, I chose to defend myself. To help me prepare my case, the army supplied me with the military law code. This tome was more than a little unnerving because, under the section detailing the different punishments that a court martial can mete out, the list included execution by firing squad. As a naturally anxious person, I immediately imagined that this was what was in store for me. I reasoned that, as they had failed to make an example out of me by solitary confinement, they were now determined to do so by firing squad! While it was possible to dispel the idea during daytime as nonsense, this was much harder when awake in the middle of the night.

Mercifully, good sense prevailed. Instead of ordering me to be shot at dawn, my second court martial did what the first might have done. Staff Sergeant Jooste signalled the outcome by driving me to court in his vintage motorcar. I sat next to him in the front seat. He said that I deserved better than the 'swart gevaar', his nickname for the black caged vehicle used to transport prisoners. I suspect that he wanted to show off his gleaming car to my supporters but it is just possible that he wanted to treat me as a civilian because by this time we had a relationship that, at a push, could pass for friendship. The brief hearing ended by convicting me on the grounds that I had disobeyed a lawful command in detention barracks. Then, deaf to my plea in mitigation of sentence, that I had pointed out at my first court martial that I was bound to refuse the order to wear military uniform, the judge sentenced me to one year in civilian prison.

The small mercy of the sentence to civilian prison was that, unlike a sentence to DB, it automatically conferred a dishonourable discharge from the South African Defence Force. The military did not want convicted criminals in its ranks. While Staaff drove me back to DB to await transfer to Pretoria Central Prison, I consoled myself with the thought that I would never be called up again.

10

PRETORIA CENTRAL

For there is no distinction; since all have sinned and fall short of the glory of God, they are justified by his grace as a gift, through the redemption which is in Christ Jesus.

(Saint Paul, 'The Epistle to the Romans')

Some twenty years after Nelson Mandela and his co-accused were tried in the Palace of Justice in Pretoria, I was driven from DB to the Palace in the 'swart gevaar'. The occasion was a hearing called to review my court martial and, if my sentence was deemed appropriate, to confirm my one-year sentence to Pretoria Central Prison. As I sat on the bench outside the court, waiting to be called in, I recalled reading about the famous Rivonia trial, which prompted an editorial in *The Times* to comment, 'The verdict of history will be that the ultimate guilty party is the government in power.'

The court wasted little time in confirming my guilt. The learned judge, an English-speaking South African, went on to rubber-stamp the sentence meted out by the court martial. In doing so he sent down a young man with no previous convictions to a notoriously dangerous prison. Furthermore, he sent me down for a whole year for a single offence of refusing a command to wear military uniform (I had paid the punishment for the others). I could not help thinking that, with just a little daring on his part, he might have pointed out that it was hardly appropriate to impose a sentence of a full year in prison for an offence that in DB had merited just two weeks in solitary confinement. But this was wishful thinking because, like Nelson Mandela, I had committed the most heinous crime of all, which was to call attention to the guilt of the apartheid state and all its officers, including those members of a so-called independent judiciary who meted out apartheid justice.

Pretoria Central Prison was top security. Not only did it house some of the most notorious prisoners in the country but it also had a special wing for political prisoners. DB would not have held many of my new fellow inmates for longer than a day. A prominent feature of prison life was the number of times we were counted each day: on waking, at our cell door, before breakfast, in the cavernous central hall, after lunch, again in the hall and then last thing at night, at our cell doors. Each time the tally had to be exactly right. Given the margin of error in the best systems, the innumeracy of the average prison warder and the vastly overcrowded prison, we spent interminable hours being counted and recounted and counted again.

The best indication of the harshness of the prison regime was that one could have eaten a meal off any floor in the entire prison. The floor in the main hall was especially impressive. This was burnished by layers of black polish to such a pitch that the few lights in the hall reflected off the floor almost as brightly as did the lights themselves. On my first morning, the prison standard was impressed upon me by a warder who took hold of my pillow, threw it under my bed and then inspected it for dust. Needless to say, I had not dusted under my bed and so spent the second night in the punishment block on bread and water. I did not make the same mistake again, and learned to make up my cell to such a high standard that, ever since, it has not been easy to share a home with an extremely untidy family; when the mess begins to overwhelm me, I find myself breaking into the cold sweat of fear.

Short-term prisoners, all those serving for one year and less, were assigned household chores, while long-term prisoners had to work in the prison factory. My first assignment was to the ablution block at the end of our corridor. The work was not arduous, save when the toilets became blocked. Then 'mucking out' could leave the block awash with urine and faeces, because the long line of prisoners, each with their cell bucket, would not hesitate to tip the contents of their bucket into the blocked and overflowing sewer. The experience of cleaning up the mess gave me to appreciate the difficult task prison warders face in maintaining basic human standards, and so I early on resolved to give them my full co-operation. Furthermore, never having performed menial tasks before, I felt I was in some small way atoning for all the chores that servants had done for me throughout my life and which I had not even noticed.

My second assignment was to the massive hall at the centre of the prison. Here the four wings of the prison, each several storeys high, met and disgorged their prisoners for roll-call. I joined a squad of four cleaners, each responsible for a quarter of the floor, which in total measured about seventy-five metres square. Our task involved maintaining the lustre of the floor by layering it with polish, brushing the polish in on all-fours, and then pulling a large, heavy polisher over the floor back and forth, back and forth, until the floor shone like a shooting star. It was good exercise and I worked with a will.

The one frustration of working in the hall was that the four cleaners had to co-operate in order to get the job done. However, co-operation was not always forthcoming and, while I had the strong incentive of study in the prison library to get the chore over with, my fellow workers had no interest whatsoever in finishing the task quickly, especially when it was cold and wet outside. Our squad therefore had interests in common but also interests that fundamentally clashed: we all wanted the job well done – in order to avoid the harsh punishment meted out for shoddy work – but, while I wanted to work efficiently, the others wanted to take as long as possible. We had to strike a compromise. I have since used what I learned from this experience in a lecture on management to illustrate the competing interests of management and employees, and the negotiation skills and incentives needed to reach a constructive agreement without resorting to throwing a punch.

The concrete courtyard of the prison was the only recreational space for over two thousand prisoners. An anthropologist would have found the range of human behaviours fascinating. The small group of body-builders at the far end stood out. These individuals effectively ran the prison on behalf of the warders. The absolute power they wielded was marked for all to see by the safe distance other prisoners kept from the space they occupied. It was also on display in their bulging biceps. While the rest of us grew progressively thinner on meagre rations, they were able to extract enough from the prison kitchen and their fellow prisoners to pump iron. Very rarely there would be a rebellion against their rule. What tended to happen was that a prisoner's self-control, which can never be relaxed in such a pressurised environment, would suddenly snap. The body-builders would push him an inch too far. The unequal contest would be over before the ever-present warders could interfere. But the violence was too awful to behold. It was so brutal and so quickly over that it did not even cross my mind to intervene.

Initially, I tried to shut myself off from the teeming mass of humanity in the yard by immersing myself in my UNISA Theology degree. I still have the book on the theology of Paul the Apostle, by the German Hermann Ridderbos, which I annotated at the time, sitting on the rim of a bath in the opposite corner of the yard to that occupied by the body-builders. It was a good setting for a study of the first great Christian theologian because the yard resonated with his view of a humanity totally cut off from God on account of sin and in desperate need of the redemption offered by Jesus Christ. I remember marvelling at his extraordinary theological profundity in imagining Jesus as the second Adam, the new creation, God's second chance for a world that rejects goodness and love. Indeed, if Paul is to be believed, the whole prison yard had already been taken up into God and restored in the death and resurrection of Christ; we simply could not see the transformation. The cosmic scope of it all was mind-blowing. As so often happens, the truth was in the contrast: in such a place, such a hope.

I also started to teach myself New Testament Greek. My progress was frustrated by the noise all about me, from which it was not possible to escape even after lock-up when music from a popular channel would be blasted throughout the prison on crackly loudspeakers. Ever since I have a loathing for DJs, whose capacity to fill dead air with an uninterrupted stream of inanities presented me with the severest mental torture. The noise, overcrowding, concrete environment and the lack of sunshine were infinitely harder to endure than anything I had encountered before. At moments I grew so frustrated that I would long to be back in the punishment cells at DB, where there were no distractions and total silence.

It quickly became apparent that most prisoners were from poor and uneducated backgrounds. They were a miserable lot, whose sense of self-worth had been so trampled upon that they seemed to shuffle along, desperately trying to avoid attracting any attention. I suspect that most of them had turned to crime because they were incapable of holding down even the most basic of the unskilled jobs reserved for poor Whites under the apartheid policy of job reservation and were too simple to plan their crimes in such a way that they escaped detection. They were the ready slaves of any prisoner bold enough to assert himself over them.

The few educated people quickly identified each other and tended to stick together. They also tended to work the system by getting themselves into the lower levels of the prison administration or library or laundry. There, like the middle classes everywhere, they made themselves indispensable and tried to accumulate small comforts which did not draw attention to themselves. However, some of them used their flair for administration to organise a variety of different activities, such as the weekly film, a chess club, a football league and the infernal prison radio.

Effeminate prisoners were claimed as mistresses by the body-builders. The openly gay ones fared better because they had learned coping strategies for dealing with the mixture of homophobia and male rape that they were threatened with each day. The saddest figure of all was a tall, old man, in his eighties, who had murdered his wife in a fit of rage. He never spoke to anyone and had the look of such black despair about him that I wondered whether even Saint Paul's gospel could reach him. With not a great deal else to do but pore over Ridderbos, I could not help being both repulsed and fascinated by my observations of this human society, especially as it had an uncanny resemblance to the so-called free society outside.

As the weeks wore on, I was challenged to get closer to my fellow prisoners. While the great missionary to the Gentiles, with his impressive evangelistic zeal, would doubtless have started a small church in the courtyard of the prison, I accepted that I was not quite so missionary-minded and simply tried to muck in and be as friendly as I could. I even went so far as to go a few rounds in the boxing ring with a prisoner before he landed one or two serious blows and I thought better of it. I played in the football league, which took place on gravel where it was lethal to fall. I liked to join the audiences of the few stand-up comedians, with their biting wit and ribald tales. Ever since, I have marvelled at their ability to lighten bleak situations by getting people to forget themselves and to experience the healing power of laughter.

A few of the educated prisoners shared their stories with me. A persistent fraudster, who had been ordered to be detained indefinitely at the State President's pleasure on account of his many crimes, was particularly entertaining because he readily confessed to not being able to keep straight and would recount with pride some of the scams he had succeeded in getting away with. A handsome young man, obviously from a good home, who had been convicted for rape and placed in the cell next to mine, was the only sex offender I encountered. He was continually mocked and asked for the graphic details of what he and his two fellow rapists had done. I once heard him sobbing that he could take no more. As there was no separate wing for sex offenders, I doubt that anyone convicted of child sexual abuse would have survived.

Occasionally, I encountered acts of unexpected human kindness. One such occurred when I had been ejected from my single cell by the prisoner in charge of our wing and sent to join two other prisoners in another single cell. I can vividly recall the moment the door was closed, and the three of us were left standing no more than a foot apart in the confined space, as one of the most fearful in my life, for there was no reason why, in this maximum security prison, one or both the prisoners might not be murderers. Stories of male rape abounded. Unless a warder chose to look in through the spy hole, there would be no witnesses. And the thick walls and door made any attempt to shout for help hopeless. In any case, the warders were unlikely to intervene. To my immense relief, instead of setting on me, the two men insisted on offering me the bed. I did take it the first night, after which we took turns to sleep on the bed, then on the floor under the bed, and then on the floor between the bed and slopping out bucket.

The night before a hanging, the prison was always tense. Once I heard singing floating on the air in the early morning coming from the block housing the political prisoners. The singing was their way of accompanying a condemned man to the scaffold. I only once entered this block when I was taken and interrogated for allegedly smuggling letters out. It was a frightening experience because the security policemen I encountered were entirely different from the average prison warder. I instinctively sensed that their way was to inflict pain, and then ask questions. The incident brought me as close as I was to get to those who were held under the same roof as me, but who were regarded as so dangerous to the security of the state that they were not even allowed to mix with murderers and other violent offenders. Whatever they had done, they certainly had acted against the evil of apartheid. I could not help admiring them.

While there is no space here to give an account of all the heroes who died and were tortured in Pretoria Central Prison, rather than allow them all to remain anonymous, I shall recall one, Solomon Kalushi Mahlangu, because he and I were the same age. But that is about all we two South Africans shared, apart from our common humanity, for the trajectory of our lives could not have been more different. He was brought up in the Mamelodi Township by his mother – a single parent. He attended Mamelodi High School, where he reached the final grade, but was unable to complete his education because of the disruption and closure of schools following the protests against Bantu education. After the Soweto riots of 16 June 1976, he joined the ANC and was sent out of the country to train as an Umkhonto we Sizwe guerrilla. After his training in Angola and Mozambique, he returned a year later as part of a group of ten smuggling in weapons, ammunition, explosives and ANC literature into the country. On 13 June 1977, just three days before the anniversary of the 16 June uprising in Soweto, he and a companion, Mondy Johannes Motloung, were accosted by police in Goch Street, Johannesburg. In the ensuing gunfight, Mondy Motloung killed two civilians.

What happened to these two after their arrest and detention in Pretoria Central Prison hardly bears thinking about. In the eyes of the police and security services, they committed the ultimate crime by shooting at police. One suggestion of the extent to which they were tortured is that by the time their case came to court in November 1977, Mondy Motloung was found unfit to stand trial as a result of mental illness. Solomon Mahlangu was convicted under the law of common purpose and was found guilty on two counts of murder and three counts under the Terrorism Act. He was sentenced to death on 2 March 1978. Despite numerous interventions on his behalf by concerned individuals, international organisations, foreign governments and the United Nations, the death sentence was carried out in Pretoria Central Prison on 6 April 1979. Solomon Mahlangu was twenty-three years old.

In contrast to the heroic resistance of political prisoners like Solomon Mahlangu, I was a mere nuisance to the apartheid regime. Nevertheless, I had the small satisfaction of knowing that I was considered sufficient of a nuisance to be denied parole. This meant that, instead of having the last quarter of my sentence waived for good behaviour, as happened with most categories of prisoner, I was made to sit out the full year in the hope that it would deter other would-be conscientious objectors. But this extra punishment was in vain because the number of objectors and those merely dodging the draft continued to increase, with an estimated quarter of the annual call-up failing to report for duty in the closing years of apartheid. This desertion of military service was more than anybody in the peace movement had hoped for. Another small cause for celebration was that, after my trial, courts martial started sentencing conscientious objectors straight to civilian prison and not to DB. They thereby escaped the order to wear military uniform and, like me, earned that rare distinction, a dishonourable discharge from the SADF.

So the year of my sentence dragged on and finally drew to a close, but not without one final unforgettable experience, my transfer from Pretoria Central Prison to Durban Central Prison for release. The journey on the back of a small, caged prison van or, as they are known in South Africa, a backie, was a terrifying finale. We started out just as the dawn was breaking and I was able to watch my first sunrise through the cage in nearly two years. I was handcuffed and manacled with leg irons to two other prisoners. The driver was a young man who drove at a furious pace, sometimes knocking the three of us into a heap on the floor of the van. It was a day's journey and we were not allowed out. One of my fellow prisoners had diarrhoea. When he needed to use the bucket provided us in the back, with the van bucking and careering about, we helped manoeuvre him onto the seat and held him there. We were all a sorry mess by the time we reached Durban. But nothing could dim the elation that stayed with me all the way from Pretoria to Durban. I was going home, I had served my time.

11

GRANDFATHER MADIBA

'He is more serene than the Dalai Lama,
more forgiving than Gandhi,
more eloquent than Churchill.
To us he is our history's miracle;
our national treasure;
You may call him Nelson Mandela.
But he is our grandfather, Madiba.'

(A popular song)

On 15 February 1983, the day of my release from prison, apartheid was still far from over. If anything it looked as entrenched as ever because, with Ronald Reagan in the White House and Margaret Thatcher in Downing Street, White supremacy in Southern Africa was supported by the Western powers as an essential bulwark against the spread of Communism in the region. Reagan and Thatcher both opposed economic sanctions and opted for a policy of 'constructive engagement' – a euphemism for encouraging cosmetic political changes to apartheid while keeping Whites in power for as long as it took to defeat Marxism. The two Western political leaders would doubtless have approved of the judgement at my court martial.

But the grievances of the African people could not be

chained up and banished forever to Robben Island. This became all too evident to me when, after an absence of two years, I emerged back into apartheid society to find that the level of violence had escalated on all sides. Security was on red alert in Durban after a terrorist bomb killed civilians in a nightclub. The law courts and police stations were ringed with barbed wire. Rioting youth were now in complete control of the townships. 'Necklacing' was a frequent occurrence. All the police and military could do was to patrol in armour-plated vehicles called Casspirs, from which they dared not dismount. The seething anger of Black people was much the same in the townships of every major South African city.

Koevoet's reign of terror continued unabated on the Namibian border. South African forces were propping up Ian Smith's White minority regime in the civil war in Rhodesia, and were actively destabilising all independent African states in the region sympathetic to the ANC by arming and fighting alongside rebel movements. Commando units were also involved in a campaign of economic sabotage that hoped to beggar South Africa's Marxist neighbours, Angola and Mozambique, by knocking out their key economic installations in order to prevent their reconstruction and development after decades of war. The talk everywhere was of a 'total onslaught' from Communist forces that had to be repulsed with the aid of a 'total strategy' linking government, the police, security services, armed forces, the media and big business.

It was sobering to reflect that I had been released from a violent prison into a society every bit as violent. With these depressing thoughts, I looked about for something useful to do that would not implicate me in the violence. But my employment prospects as an ex-convict were bleak. There was no possibility of being employed in one of the public sector economic development corporations, which I had proposed as an alternative to military service. The diocese of Namibia had filled my former post with an American missionary, so there was no going back there. Mercifully, Archbishop Hurley and

Paddy Kearney provided me with an opportunity to escape from the Whites only side of town during working hours by asking me to direct the ecumenical centre which was planned to provide new offices for Diakonia, a Christian resources centre and conference venue, and a base for the broad coalition of anti-apartheid organisations in Durban supportive of the United Democratic Front (UDF).

The formation of the UDF was a reaction to the increasingly isolated apartheid regime's divide and rule tactics. In a last desperate attempt to hang on to power, the government had created alliances with moderate Black leaders in the hope of drawing support away from the African National Congress and the smaller Pan African Congress and South African Communist Party, all three of which were banned as terrorist organisations but which nonetheless enjoyed popular support. Homeland leaders, such as KwaZulu's Chief Mangosuthu Buthelezi, were courted and promised special privileges in a proposed confederation of political units into which the country was to be divided. The so-called Coloured and Indian population groups were invited to join a tri-cameral parliament, which enlarged the formerly Whites only parliament by creating three separate chambers for each of the European, Coloured and Asian groups. This brazen attempt to co-opt Indians and Coloureds on the side of apartheid so enraged progressives in all communities that they united with civic organisations, trade unions and religious bodies to form the UDF.

Between 1983 and 1988, when the UDF was finally banned, the beleaguered government responded by a wave of repression. Thousands of government opponents were detained without trial. Troops were sent into the townships to quell unrest. Successive states of emergency were declared from 1985 until the end of the decade. The situation was not sustainable. Seeing the writing on the wall, a delegation of senior business leaders, led by Gavin Relly, Chairman of the giant Anglo American Corporation, flew to the ANC headquarters in Lusaka, Zambia, in an attempt to broker a deal between the Nationalist government and the ANC. At the same time, the more enlightened of the Afrikaner nationalists explored the release of Nelson Mandela from life imprisonment on condition that he renounce violence.

There were also humiliating setbacks in South Africa's military forays from Namibia into Angola. Keen to be seen to be protecting Western interests in Angola, where the Marxist Movement for the Popular Liberation of Angola (MPLA) had seized power from the former Portuguese colonial rulers and were engaged in a prolonged civil war with the rival pro-Western liberation movement, UNITA, South African troops invaded Angola. Russia and Cuba responded by sending arms, logistical support and then troops in support of their Angolan ally. The use of Russian MiG 23 jet fighters, piloted by Angolans and Cubans and far superior to South Africa's ancient Mirage planes, proved to be decisive in the battle for Cuito Cuanavale in 1986. A battalion of South Africa's crack troops were pinned down and were eventually forced to retreat after suffering heavy losses in what has been described as Africa's largest battle since El Alamein. From this date, the hitherto invincible South African army was on the defensive and was gradually withdrawn from Angola and then from Namibia itself.

Back in South Africa, no amount of state-sponsored violence could hold back the turning tide. In addition to the crippling cost of maintaining its army of occupation in Namibia, international economic sanctions, particularly on oil, placed an impossible burden on the economy. The withdrawal of foreign investment and the declining price of gold put paid to the hope that South Africa could provide employment for its exploding and explosive Black population. Student activists had made the townships ungovernable, making it impossible for local authorities to collect rates and taxes. Public utilities were also unable to extract payment for supplying electricity, water and telephone. The trade unions became increasingly militant, adding to the fears of international corporations and investors. Meanwhile, Umkhonto we Sizwe, the military wing of the exiled African National Congress, extended its campaign of sabotage.

With even the military beginning to question the sustainability of apartheid, the most *kragdadig*, or rightwing, Afrikaner politician was forced to rethink his views on terrorism. The reformers in the Cabinet, under the leadership of F.W. de Klerk, wrestled power from the embattled P.W. Botha, whose only response to the cycle of violence had been more of the same. Then, in 1990, with no better hope than Nelson Mandela, the Nationalist government released him unconditionally to prepare for South Africa's first free elections. The government also took the once unthinkable step of unbanning the ANC, PAC and even the SACP. Four momentous years later, Nelson Mandela led the ANC to a resounding victory to become the first democratically elected President of South Africa.

What was altogether remarkable about the end was how relatively peacefully the transfer of power to the Black majority came about. The dire predictions of rivers of blood failed to materialise. The new government adopted a responsible approach to the economy and quietly shelved, as a relic of the Cold War, the wholesale nationalisations promised in the Freedom Charter. The fears of the minority White population that they would be stripped of their wealth and driven into the sea proved to be unfounded.

Much of the credit must go to Nelson Mandela, whom Whites soon could not believe they had imprisoned as the leader of a terrorist organisation. He was as magnanimous in victory as he had been unwavering in his commitment to refuse freedom on any ground other than the complete dismantling of apartheid. Deservedly, in a world grown cynical of its political leaders, he shone as a beacon of integrity. But more than that, this incredibly youthful old man, who had missed out on so much in twenty-seven years of prison, emerged without rancour or bitterness as a reconciler.

Of Nelson Mandela's many speeches and gestures, the one which completely won over rugby-mad White South Africans was his donning of the Springbok rugby jersey to congratulate his victorious team in the World Cup Final of 1995, in which the Springboks beat the All Blacks. It was a rare moment in which politics and sport combined to promote national unity in the way the Olympic games united the warring Greek city-states. Only Black South Africans can know the personal cost to their new President because the Springbok rugby jersey in the apartheid era was reserved for Whites only and Blacks were barred from attending test matches in case they shouted for the opposing side. After the uniforms of the South African police and military, it was a potent symbol of the brutality of Afrikanerdom.

But Nelson Mandela's personal moral authority cannot on its own explain the miracle. With him out of jail, it was still touch and go at times. In the run up to the election, the bitter struggle for supremacy in KwaZulu and Natal between his ANC supporters and those of Chief Buthelezi's Inkatha Freedom Party spread to the Reef. The conflict spilled out into the streets of Johannesburg itself. In the townships Zulu impis, armed with traditional assegais and knobkerries as well as Russian AK-47 rifles and homemade guns manufactured in the hostels, clashed with ANC self-defence units, armed with AK-47s and grenades. The Machiavellian tactics of the outgoing White regime seized on the mayhem to pit Black against Black in what it hoped would be a fight to the death. For a while the terrifying ghosts of warlords, such as Shaka, seemed to have risen to stalk the land.

What saved the day was the depth of leadership in civil society. This forced the political parties to draw up the National Peace Accord, signed by the main political leaders in Johannesburg on 14 September 1991. The Accord committed the parties to a non-violent path to democracy, and to participate in structures through which this commitment could be monitored and implemented. For the next three years, the

National Peace Committee with its highly active secretariat, its eleven Regional Peace Committees and, by 1994, two hundred and sixty Local Peace Committees, worked steadily towards the first fully democratic election by bringing political leaders together with representatives from the churches, business, community groups and the security forces in a continuous process of peace building.

The Accord held because it provided an accessible forum for all levels of society in which anger could be vented, violence investigated, disputes mediated, relief and reconstruction planned, and understanding and co-operation forged. The peace committees also trained an estimated two hundred thousand local peace monitors. Crucially, they also engaged the township youth, who might otherwise have disrupted the process. Many of them were trained as peace monitors and they played an important and constructive role on polling day with their distinctive peace uniforms. The international community also gave unstinting support by contributing hundreds of observers from the UN, Commonwealth, European Union and OAU to the peace structures.

The outstanding figure in civil society at this critical time was Desmond Tutu. He had survived BOSS's attempt to implicate him in the financial mismanagement of the South African Council of Churches and had used the Eloff Commission of investigation into the Council as a platform to deliver a stinging denunciation of apartheid. His courageous leadership earned him the Nobel Peace Prize in 1984. Later that year, he was elected Bishop of Johannesburg, but served for little more than a year before he was elected Archbishop of Cape Town in 1986. As *Mbhishobhi Omkhulu*, or great bishop, he used his office to campaign tirelessly for peace. In the run up to the elections, he often left the safety of the Archbishop's Palace in Cape Town to mediate between the Nationalist Government, the ANC and Inkatha, to lead protest marches, and to take funerals of the victims of township violence. He would not hesitate to wade fearlessly and alone into outbreaks of violence to impose calm.

The new South Africa was fortunate to have in Desmond Tutu a leader who was both beyond politics and no one's 'sycophantic lickspittle'. President Nelson Mandela, after a landslide victory, soon found himself being criticised for presiding over a new government of national unity that wasted little time before awarding itself large increases in pay. Tutu mocked the new MPs for slowing down the gravy train only for long enough to jump on. For his pains, the new government reacted uncommonly like the old one by ordering him to keep out of politics and to stick to religion. However, with his fierce independence, infectious joy, irrepressible humour, international reputation and upbringing in a township, he was the 'people's archbishop' – far too popular a figure to ignore.

Nelson Mandela was too gracious a leader to take the criticism personally and made the inspired decision to appoint Desmond Tutu to head the Truth and Reconciliation Commission (TRC), a national structure set up to promote reconciliation after the elections. The TRC provided a creative outlet for the potentially destructive rage of apartheid's victims by enabling them to tell their stories, recording them and producing an account for all future generations of what it took for South Africans to be free. The Commission also invited all who had committed human rights abuses, and who, it was feared, would seek to avoid punishment for their crimes by attempting to overthrow the fragile new state, to confess their crimes as a condition for qualifying for amnesty. This very Christian fusion of forgiveness and pragmatism presented a novel response to the conundrum of how to break the cycle of violence and bring about justice in the still extremely violent and politically polarised post-apartheid situation. Although the Commission's work did not please everyone, the recording of the victims' stories and the public shaming of their tormentors helped to consolidate the process of nation building started by the National Peace Accord. Desmond Tutu hoped the end result would be a 'rainbow people', his description of a nation that rejoices in its diversity and is at peace with itself.

As for the continuation of my story while these historic events were unfolding, Alison joined me as soon as she could after my release from prison for the two weeks of her Easter holidays. We spent much of the time at my parents' cottage, Spurwing, set in a bird sanctuary on the shores of the Albert Falls reservoir outside Pietermaritzburg. The bright-yellow weavers, chattering away in their nests in the branches overhanging the cottage roof, were an especially friendly presence. Out walking along the shore, we raised flocks of bishop birds, with the distinctive males sporting their red breasts and long black tails. In the evenings we sat on the veranda, waiting for the Spurwing geese to come honking in to land on the water. When the wind came up, Alison took me sailing on my brother's catamaran. I took her riding. It was the perfect setting for a wonderfully soothing and relaxing holiday for two people living on the edge: she in her first experience of hospital medicine and me adjusting to life on the outside.

The only pressure on us was the decision we needed to make about our future together. This was complicated by the fact that Alison would qualify as a doctor in the summer, and then was required to work a further three years in Britain's National Health Service before she would be eligible for a partnership in general practice. I was committed to the 'struggle' against apartheid and could not contemplate leaving South Africa. Alison offered to give up her hopes to be a GP in the NHS and to come and live in South Africa. Having experienced the end of White rule in one country, Basutoland, and its descent into a violent dictatorship and economic chaos, I worried that South Africa's uncertain future and high level of violent crime made the sacrifice too great. We discussed the possibility of children and wondered what prospects they would have as White South Africans.

Matters came to a head in the last few days of the holiday,

after a visit to the arboretum and formal gardens on the nearby Giekie estate. We took a basket of tea with us and spread a blanket in the shade of the magnificent rhododendron bushes for which the garden is well known. That evening, as I was preparing for supper, Alison burst in to my room after a bath in some alarm to say that she was covered in microscopic black spots that were not coming off. When we managed to prise one off her skin and look at it under a magnifying glass, the black body and legs of a baby tick were unmistakable. Gorged on the blood of its host, the mature tick can grow to the size of a large button. Worse, tick bite fever can be fatal. Alison must have lain on a nest of ticks because she was infested from head to toe. We had to get them off.

This was a delicate predicament for which evangelical Christianity proved inadequate. We were alone in the cottage. There was no one but me to help remove the ticks. When Alison eventually grasped what had to be done, she removed her bathrobe and dived, face down, on to my bed. I conducted a painstakingly thorough examination with my patient giggling into the pillow. Afterwards, sitting on the veranda, with the chattering of the weaver birds overhead, and having not yet settled whether we would live in England or South Africa, we set a date for our wedding later that year.

12

LIFE TOGETHER

Busie old foole, unruly Sunne
Why dost thou thus,
Through windowes, and through curtains call on us?

(John Donne, *The Sunne Rising*)

The impossible part of playing the hero is the expectation that one can sustain the part indefinitely. I was not up to it, especially after Alison left me to complete her last six months of hospital house jobs in London. After the two years I had spent in prison, the two precious weeks we spent together at Spurwing seemed agonisingly incomplete. She had somehow managed to pierce through all the levels of self-containment I had built up as armour-plating against the ugly world outside. For a brief, intense moment we belonged together. Her conversation, her soft touch, her dear face, had transported me beyond the lingering nightmares of prison, DB and courts martial, and I had been momentarily able to forget, to relax and to enjoy another person's company. With her gone, the reality of apartheid South Africa came flooding back and now overwhelmed me.

In a thoroughly depressed state of mind, with my work at the Ecumenical Centre bringing me into daily contact with the victims of the state and township violence, I endlessly turned over the question Alison and I had left unresolved about our future. I wondered how I could possibly justify bringing my English lady to live in a country where young people liked to chant 'one settler one bullet' and mean it. But having left South Africa once before and having gone through all I had since my return, I could not contemplate leaving a second time. I believed I had to stay and be part of the 'struggle'. Besides I was now a prisoner of conscience and such a hero does not cut and run.

An incident at the Ecumenical Centre then precipitated a shameful decision. Arriving early one morning, I was threatened by one of the many vagrants who searched through the city each day for work. The desperate man turned on me after I had to refuse his pleading to join the gang of labourers our builder had hired from the army of unemployed at the official city labour exchange. He was in a sorry state and so I was probably never in any serious danger. Nevertheless, the trivial incident, combining with the township violence and my trough of despond, decided me that the situation was hopeless. I lost my nerve and telephoned Alison to call off our marriage. It was a difficult, confused and lonely time, and made more so because Alison sounded so terribly upset.

At this low ebb, the new Bishop of Natal, Michael Nuttall, came to our aid. Hoping that I might discover a vocation to the priesthood, he helped me apply to Oxford University to complete the degree in Theology, which I had started with UNISA in prison. Balliol College, known for supporting progressive causes, found me a place, an honour I would never have merited on academic grounds alone. With the prospect of seeing Alison again, life suddenly took on a brighter aspect. The future would simply have to take care of itself.

Our wedding took place five days before the start of the Oxford University term. The service was held at St Nicholas's, a quaint Norman church built in 1140 out of pudding stone, in Pyrford, Surrey. I warmed to the church even more when I learned that it was associated with the poet John Donne, who after secretly marrying his under-age Anne, was imprisoned in the Fleet for a year by his father-in-law.

Father Paul Hume (SSM), who baptised me as a child in Teyateyaneng, gave the blessing. Ken Costa acted as my best man. Apart from my parents and some retired former District Commissioners in Basutoland, the guests were almost entirely Alison's family and friends from St Helen's. It was difficult to sense what they made of her South African husband and recent inmate of Pretoria Central Prison, but I remember the reception as a happy occasion, when everyone genuinely seemed to wish us well.

After a short honeymoon in an oasthouse in Kent, lent to us by Alison's Aunt Sybil, we moved to the delightfully named Tinkerbell Cottage, on Boars Hill outside Oxford. I was not to know that Boars Hill was regarded as the somewhat exclusive haunt of Oxford academics. However, whereas they all lived in substantial houses, our first home was a cosy one up and one down terraced cottage, with a freezing cold bathroom, where the condensation was so thick one could barely see the other end of the bath. It was a good home in which to learn to live together because the cramped conditions forced us into close contact and, as there was only ever enough hot water for one bath, we took to bathing together – a simple formula for an enduring marriage.

Another cementing pastime was Alison reading aloud to me last thing at night. Our first book was Roland Bainton's biography of Martin Luther, *Here I Stand*. After ploughing through this worthy book for my sake, Alison decided that Church history was best kept for study hours and settled for the wartime romance by H.E. Bates, *Fair Stood the Wind for France*. Another early favourite was Kenneth Grahame's, *The Wind in the Willows*, with Alison giving each of the main characters, Ratty, Mole, Badger and Toad, a distinctive voice. Alison's reading has been a marvellous introduction to English literary culture for me, and it is surprising what one can get through over the years. Although her books did not yet exist at this time, J.K. Rowling's delightful little heroine, Hermione Grainger, the companion of Harry Potter, perfectly described how I pictured my new wife as a girl – annoyingly intelligent, invariably right, maddeningly obsessive, but utterly dependable and ever so attractive.

Alison wisely took six months off from medicine to adjust to her demanding new husband. And I took a lot of adjusting to. I had only ever lived in institutions which served me three meals a day. I had also lived in the five-star establishment run by my grandmother. It was therefore as much as I could do to boil a kettle and make a cup of tea. I was a total stranger to washing up. This particular household chore proved the first point of friction between us when, recalling Carmel Rickard's lectures at Diakonia on equal marriage, I manfully volunteered to do the dishes. On the first attempt I slaved away through a great mountain of plates, pots, cutlery and glasses, only to find Alison later pointedly re-washing all the glasses. When I failed again on my second attempt, Alison delivered the first of many lectures on domestic affairs. The form of the lecture never varies. It begins with a methodical description of exactly what is required of me; this is repeated so that I cannot claim to have misunderstood; finally, the message is underlined, leaving me quaking in my boots.

What with learning how to obey my wife – in all things – and trying to understand the confusing minds of Oxford theology dons there was no let-up for me. The immediate academic challenge was to master New Testament Greek in order to read the four Gospels and Paul's Epistle to the Romans in the original text. While Alison slept, I was forced to keep South African hours by working on my Greek from six till seven-thirty each morning. I then served Alison tea and breakfast in bed, before battling through the Oxford rush-hour traffic to get to my first lecture. The rest of the day would be spent in the Radcliffe Camera or some other temple of learning, where I would research and then write a weekly essay for my tutor. For that exhausting first term, this was the forgiving

Father Ian Brayley, a Jesuit at Campion Hall. When I had read through my essay, parts of which he really did sleep through, he would hand out the next week's topic with an intimidating list of about thirty books of recommended reading. Needless to say, I had two left feet by the evening when Alison joined me for a ballroom dancing class. After a few weeks we conceded the floor to the rest of our class of unmarried undergraduates, who gave the impression of only rising at midday and partying all night.

In addition to providing the space for Alison and me to begin life as husband and wife away from the tense conflict in South Africa, Oxford offered an opportunity to try to sort out my muddled thinking on war. With the prosecution's questions at my first court martial ringing in my ears, I sat with burning curiosity through a paper on the theory of the just war, taught by Oliver O'Donovan, Professor of Moral and Pastoral Theology, in his study overlooking Tom Quad at Christ Church. The paper took me on a guided tour of all the main contributors down the ages: the early African Bishop of Hippo, Augustine, who wrote in response to the Barbarian threat to Roman civilisation, the Scholastic Aquinas, known affectionately as the Angelic Doctor for his voluminous writings and commanding influence over the Roman Catholic Church, the stern Protestant reformer, Calvin, the Counter-Reformation Spaniards Victoria and Saurez, and modern theologians, such as the American Paul Ramsay. The thrust of the paper was that the just war tradition was conceived and developed to prevent the outbreak of war and to limit its ferocity.

While the paper led me to accept that the tradition presented the only rational framework for judging the rights and wrongs of war, I still could not help wondering whether David Jenkins, the former Bishop of Durham, was closer to the truth in one of his witticisms when he says, 'There is no such thing as a *just* war, one just has to go to war sometimes.' I also continued to think it important to affirm the pacifist witness, especially as nearly two Christian millennia culminated in the saturation bombing of London and Dresden and the dropping of atomic bombs on Hiroshima and Nagasaki by the leading Christian nations. A gripping student performance in St John's College gardens of that serious farce *Oh! What a Lovely War*, which lampoons the European nations for finding it more difficult to avoid the Great War than to start it, deepened this conviction.

I was given a further opportunity to explore the dilemma presented by war at the end of my finals in 1985, a brutal and terrifying intellectual challenge consisting of ten papers, all taken in one week. The Master of Balliol, the distinguished philosopher and former Roman Catholic priest Anthony Kenny, invited Alison and me to attend a week-long reading party on the morality of nuclear deterrence. This was held at the college's chalet in the Alps, which a former student and later Archbishop of Canterbury, William Temple, burnt down by accident on his honeymoon. While the reading party was mostly light-hearted, the seriousness of our topic occasionally impressed itself upon us and made me aware that life in Britain was potentially far more dangerous than it was even in South Africa. If deterrence failed, Britain might literally be blotted out.

We spent the morning reading, the afternoon walking and the evenings debating a collection of essays, one of which Anthony Kenny contributed with the provocative title 'Better Red Than Dead'. From what I could make of his position, while he insisted that any use of nuclear weapons is absolutely wrong, he wanted them kept as a deterrent because an enemy will not know for certain whether they will be used or not. I thought it a subtle response to the dilemma posed by the existence of weapons of mass destruction because, while acknowledging that there is no possible moral justification for their use, it recognises that the principle of mutually agreed destruction is not irrational or mad.

The other memorable part of the summer of 1985 was our visit to Taizé, the ecumenical community, founded by Brother

Roger in the South of France. It was the perfect antidote to the hard-nosed realism of nuclear deterrence. Alison and I camped alongside the host of young and not so young people drawn from all over Europe. We worshipped in the great tent and sang the special chants of the community. We prayed for the peace of the world and gave thanks for our Christian heritage. Brother Roger pictured this for us by lighting a candle and then asked each member of the vast congregation, each of whom had been issued with a candle, to receive the light and pass it on to their neighbour. Sitting at the back of the darkened hall, I remember watching entranced as the wave of light, seemingly carried on the voices of angels, washed towards me.

At the end of our summer travels, Alison and I returned to Oxford, where, having accepted that the priesthood was the next big step in my life after marriage, I was due to start training as a Church of England ordinand. Of the three Oxford training colleges, in preference to Cuddesdon, which she regarded as too liberal and too far out of town, and St Stephen's House or 'Staggers', which she regarded as too catholic and too gay, Alison chose Wycliffe Hall, the evangelical college, for me. She took seriously the responsibility that her husband should receive an orthodox and evangelical training and had been informed by her St Helen's friends that Wycliffe could be relied upon to give me a thorough grounding in a biblical Christianity. Most important of all, she was told that it would ensure I did not emerge wearing a black clerical shirt and dog collar on every conceivable occasion, including holidays, and expect everyone to call me 'Father'. I submitted willingly enough but then nearly backed out when the first college meal of term brought back all my worst memories of boarding school.

This time though Alison was by my side and, having never boarded herself, was excited by the prospect of two whole years of a common life. She even attended some of my lectures, doubtless to ensure that I was not being led astray; not that there was any risk of that with the conservative evangelical

Geoffrey Shaw as Principal and the brilliant Reformation scholar Alistair McGrath as the Senior Lecturer in Theology. Despite the college's narrow evangelical tradition, I was impressed by my fellow ordinands, who did not easily fit the mould of the stodgy, Bible-thumping evangelical clergyman. They and their spouses ensured that Alison and I enjoyed a wide range of extracurricular activities. I especially remember endless bouts of strenuous squash with Nicky Gumbel, who left to promote, with Ken Costa and others at Holy Trinity Brompton, the hugely successful evangelistic initiative Alpha. With such a talented, lively and committed Christian missionary community, one had the impression that the future of the Church of England had to be rosy.

While my contemporaries trained to rescue the Church of England, I had a very different agenda. While they were preparing for a future in the northern hemisphere, I concentrated my efforts on understanding the theology emerging in the southern hemisphere and, in particular, liberation theology. This creative fusion of Christianity with Marxism originated as a response to social injustices in South America and then spread to other developing countries. In South Africa it influenced the authors of the Kairos Document and a younger generation of Black Anglican clergy working or studying abroad, such as Barney Pityana, the Director of the controversial Programme to Combat Racism at the World Council of Churches. After meeting the fiery Barney, I realised that, if I was ever to work with Black Christians like him, it was important for me to understand liberation theology and its critics, who claimed that it misunderstood Marxism and represented a dangerous type of Christian millenarianism.

I also took the opportunity of my training to write a booklet on the morality of economic sanctions. This was then the subject of intense debate in South Africa between opponents of economic sanctions, such as Alan Paton, who feared that their imposition would have a disproportionate impact on the Black population, and advocates, such as Archbishop Desmond

Tutu, who saw them as a necessary evil. With two of my great heroes on either side of the debate, and knowing what I did about the mass unemployment in South Africa, the issue presented an agonising moral dilemma. In the end I came down on the side of targeted economic sanctions on the strength of pleas by representative Black leaders, such as Archbishop Tutu, who insisted that Blacks be allowed to decide how much they were prepared to suffer to get rid of apartheid. However, I wanted the international community also to promise economic aid after the end of apartheid to enable reconstruction and development, along the lines of the Marshal Aid supplied by the United States to Western Europe at the end of the Second World War.

When the booklet was published, I sent a copy to the President of the Anti-apartheid Movement, Bishop Trevor Huddleston. At the time, he was vigorously campaigning for economic sanctions against South Africa from his base in retirement in the Vicarage at St James's Church, Piccadilly. He replied and invited me to meet him there. It was the first time I had seen him in the flesh. With the resolute set of his jaw and the extreme asceticism of his tall figure, he was every bit the image of the Old Testament prophet I had been led to expect. When it was time for me to go, we knelt and prayed in his sparsely furnished room for the release of all South African political prisoners, many of whom were known to him personally from his days as a missionary priest in Sophiatown, outside Johannesburg. It was somehow purifying to encounter such a dedicated life.

While I studied theology amidst the dreaming spires of Oxford University, Alison did something altogether more practical. She lived it. She chose to use her medical training in a clinic for homeless people, of whom there were a surprising number in Oxford. They found the city a welcome haven in the winter on account of the many large college boiler rooms. Students were also known to be a soft touch. Some let tramps sleep in their digs. Most of the homeless, though, slept rough and, over years of deprivation, developed the most appalling medical conditions. Alison, along with the other workers at the Luther Street Clinic, ministered to this lost community with such a genuine concern for their wellbeing that it made an impression on even the most hardened. I was made aware of this when, out walking with Alison, we would hear a gruff 'Ullo Doc' coming from the depths of some shelter or park bench.

Alison escaped her rough patients by joining the Oxford Bach Choir. She was keen that I should gain an appreciation of classical music and was shocked to hear that the only classical concert I had attended was a performance of Tchaikovsky's *1812 Overture* by the Durban City Orchestra, when I was an undergraduate at the University of Natal. Shortly after this concert, the orchestra was closed through a lack of support. Alison's concerts now made up for this cultural desert. I hugely enjoyed each occasion, and was terribly proud of my wife in the massed ranks of such a prestigious choir in her long black skirt, white blouse and Titian hair. Of her many concerts, the one that stands out for me was a performance of William Walton's *Belshazzar's Feast* in the Sheldonian Theatre. At the dramatic moment when the hand is seen to write on the wall, I thought of the apartheid regime: *mene*, your days are numbered; *tekel*, you have been weighed in the balance and found wanting; *upharsin*, your kingdom will be divided.

Alison also decided that we should begin our family at this time. We were determined, whatever our future, that our children should start out with British citizenship. This decision effectively meant that we were committed to living in Britain for the next few years because Alison was keen that we should have at least two children. After what seemed an inordinate wait, in which Alison grew larger and larger, on 15 February 1987 the same day and month I was released from prison four years before, Katie burst into the world. From her first day, she appeared to have inherited the tireless energy of her great-grandmother, so we gave her as her second name Joy.

We scarcely had time to get over the sleepless nights Katie inflicted on us before I was ordained at St Paul's Cathedral in the Diocese of London. As I sat under the magnificent Byzantine dome, with its chapel dedicated to the Order of the British Empire in the crypt below, I reflected that it was my grandmother's churchgoing and the example of the missionary priests at Teyateyaneng, which had set me on the path to ordination. I hoped that they were all smiling. I could not help thinking that, having been brought up at the very outer reaches of the British Empire, here I was at its very centre.

From the ordination service at St Paul's, it was up the City Road to the parish of St Mary's, Islington, with its large, diverse and supportive congregation. I was especially pleased to serve my curacy or ministerial apprenticeship at St Mary's because it fell within the Stepney area of the Diocese of London, where Trevor Huddleston had been Bishop. Stepney was and still is home to many immigrant and exiled communities, and I immediately felt very much at home in this part of London. It was not long before I found myself working with the youth of the exuberant and colourful Afro-Caribbean community, who attended the St Mary's neighbourhood centre. I helped the Youth Worker take a group of them on an unforgettable skiing holiday to a resort in Austria, which must still be recovering from the onslaught.

Our clergy apartment, just off the City Road, was large enough for us to accommodate a succession of lodgers, guests and, for a time, a family of South African refugees. It was also central enough for South African friends and acquaintances visiting London to drop in on us. So we never felt very far from the South African community. At times it was too busy for Alison, on whom I placed the impossible demand of entertaining a constant stream of parishioners, looking after Katie, giving birth in 1989 to our son, James, and keeping her medical career going. Looking back on it all now, I wonder how Alison coped and am ashamed at how much I expected of her at home while I pranced about doing noble things in the parish. It was certainly not the equal marriage Carmel had tutored me in and, had she known, she would have delivered a strong rebuke.

Many months after our move to Islington, I discovered that the parish boundary of St Mary's included the nondescript London offices of the African National Congress. Not wanting to draw undue attention to themselves in a country where they might become targets of British racists, the ANC did not advertise their presence. Following attacks by South African government agents at their other offices abroad, the building was heavily boarded up, giving it the appearance of the kind of 'adult' shop that a young clergyman ought not to be seen in. True to my profession, I passed by on several occasions with averted eyes, not knowing that my fellow countrymen were within. I was therefore surprised when an exiled member of the ANC, based in the Islington office, approached me to lead an early morning vigil outside the South African Embassy for a political prisoner condemned to die in Pretoria Central Prison. As our small group of protesters waited in Trafalgar Square for the time of his execution, I recalled the haunting sound of singing before an execution. Then, just before it was the time, one of us started to sing.

The Canon Collins Trust, with its extensive archive of documents and photographs recording the history of the anti-apartheid struggle, was a much more visible presence in the parish. Thanks to the money raised by John and Mary Collins and their fellow trustees, the legal expenses of many South African activists were met by British sympathisers. They were thereby afforded a public trial with lawyers to defend them. The trust also provided financial assistance to the families of convicted political prisoners. This helped many survive the loss of a crucial breadwinner. It also provided them with travel grants to visit their loved ones in prison. Winnie Mandela, for instance, was enabled to make several visits to see her famous husband over the long twenty-seven years of the separation that was to prove fatal to their marriage. The trust advertised itself with a display in a street window. I ventured in on only one occasion but was so sickened by the exhibits of massacred and tortured Black South Africans that, to my shame, I never returned.

My main involvement with South Africa over these three years was through the link between the Stepney area in the Diocese of London and the Diocese of Namibia. The idea behind the diocesan link was that the church should move away from a traditional missionary model, which sent British Christians to poorer countries, to a partnership model, which recognises that poorer countries also have much to contribute to the increasingly secular West. In keeping with this new approach, links between dioceses involved exchanges in both directions, so that mission became a two-way traffic. It meant, to my delight, that I got to meet in Stepney a number of the priests I had met in Namibia.

In addition to these contacts with my fellow Africans, Islington presented an interesting exposure to the changing English society of the late 1980s. The borough, once populated mainly by the working class, was becoming increasingly fashionable and yuppyfied. Its proximity to the City of London, the Inns of Court and Fleet Street meant that it was a good base for persons working in financial institutions, the legal profession and journalism. St Mary's worked hard to provide a community for all classes within its parish. Even more impressively, it reached out to embrace the many homeless people in the borough by converting its crypt into a night shelter. This radical outreach did not exactly improve the appearance of the building when the homeless took to dossing down and urinating on the porch, but it was important as a sign of the inclusiveness of the Kingdom of God. It also provided an opportunity for some of those earning astronomical salaries in the City to demonstrate a practical concern for the less fortunate.

I used to cycle down the City Road occasionally to meet some of our high-flying parishioners working in the City. This brought an important new interest and direction for my life because it brought to my attention the spate of business scandals that broke following the deregulation and global-isation of the financial services industry associated with the Thatcher revolution. Having considered my earlier under-graduate and postgraduate studies in economics and finance something of an embarrassment as well as a complete waste of time, for I saw no prospect of ever using them, I now discovered that these too had a part to play in God's economy by providing me with a basis to engage with the subject of business ethics. At the time, this new academic discipline was being pioneered by the Jesuit Jack Mahoney, the author of *The Making of Moral Theology*, a penetrating and revealing history of the development of Catholic moral teaching, who was later appointed the first Professor of Business Ethics at the London Business School.

I was keen to develop this new interest for the reason that the role of big business in helping prop up apartheid and then in helping to negotiate its end had alerted me to the increasingly dominant role of large corporations in the modern world. By this time, with talk of Nelson Mandela's imminent release, I also realised that it was important for me to try to prepare for a future beyond apartheid, where I would be called on to engage with an increasingly corporate world, where large businesses, such as General Motors, controlled economic resources many times greater than most of the world's govern-ments. With the encouragement of the Bishop of Stepney, Jim Thompson, who as a qualified accountant had a strong interest himself in business ethics, I enrolled part-time in Professor Mahoney's degree course. This led, at the end of my three-year curacy in 1990, to an invitation to join a new Ethics Institute in Oxford as a research fellow in business ethics.

The move back to Oxford in 1990 was a welcome oppor-tunity to regroup as a family and to plan our next step. With the addition of our son, James, I hoped our family was now complete and assumed that we would soon begin the move back to South Africa. After two years in which Alison revelled in having her home and family all to herself, this decision was focused for us by an invitation to become the Warden of the small Anglican theological college attached to the National University of Lesotho and to act as Anglican Chaplain to the university. I was immediately attracted by the possibility of working in the country where I was brought up and where I could speak the local African language. I also remembered Roma, the former Roman Catholic seminary, as a wonderfully scenic setting for a small African university. I therefore persuaded Alison to fly out with me to look it over, and to bring Katie and James.

I took the opportunity of the visit to show my family Teyateyaneng. It was the first part of the shattering of a dream, because we found virtually nothing intact of the little English village from my time there as a child. All the English missionaries had left, leaving behind a struggling church, close to collapse. The spacious gardens of the former residence of the British District Commissioner, which once boasted a cross country course, had simply vanished. The Country Club, which used to support a quarterly newsletter of some five pages, was empty and looked as if it had been looted. Its grounds, to which my grandparents had devoted so much of their time and had kept immaculately tidy, had large weeds growing where the tennis courts and bowling green once stood. My first home was inhabited by an Indian family, who had built a high security fence around the property. The former houses of my other relations were occupied by either Indian or Chinese families and were similarly fortified.

We were told that much the same changes had taken place throughout Lesotho. Virtually all the British expatriate families, who used to run trading stations scattered about the Maluti Mountains, had been replaced by Indian and Chinese traders. In the capital city of Maseru, the Chinese had established several clothing factories and were rumoured to control much of the commerce. Worryingly, resentment of the Chinese had sparked race riots, in which BaSotho attacked

Chinese and burnt down their businesses. Much of the city centre had been burnt. Lesotho was definitely not the Basutoland of my youth.

When we visited Roma, the atmosphere of the university was more positive. The academic buildings were comfortingly familiar. The grounds were fairly well maintained. The members of the teaching faculty and the students we met were bright and interesting. I started to think of all the things we might do. But then we were taken to the local Roman Catholic mission hospital, where Alison was told that the only doctor had just left and would she mind stepping in. Somewhat taken back by the responsibility of single-handedly running a four hundred bed hospital, when she was barely out of medical school with two small children in tow and with the grim spectre of HIV/AIDS already looming, she lamely asked whether the hospital had a policy on family planning and the use of condoms, to which she received the firm reply, 'No, because the Pope forbids it.'

Worse was still to come. On our return from Roma to Teyateyaneng, where we were staying with the Tullys, who were stubbornly refusing to leave Lesotho, we encountered the first of two roadblocks and the intractable politics of the little kingdom. The regime of Lebua Jonathan, who had ruled as one more African despot since he had lost the first general election in 1970, was expecting an attack from members of the Lesotho Liberation Army and had ordered a search of all cars on the roads. I was ordered out of the car by soldiers toting machine guns. They threatened to impound the car. I was told to drive it off the road and was ordered out again. We had been warned that police and soldiers were known to steal cars and I suspect that we were about to be the next victims. However, I was not unduly ruffled as all my memories of the BaSotho were of a gentle, peace-loving people. I spoke to the soldiers in what Sotho I could remember to explain that I had brought my family to see where I had been brought up. After what seemed an endless wait, an officer appeared and, hearing me speak

Sotho, engaged me in a long conversation about England, where he hoped to attend a military training course. After catching up with British affairs, he let me return to the car and drive on.

Alison had remained in the car all this while, with two small children and the windows tightly wound up. Unencumbered by the past, she was able to see more clearly what the BaSotho, armed with automatic weapons, had become. When we drove on, she let out a huge sigh of relief. But this was not quite the end of our African safari. We had barely travelled ten miles further down the road when we encountered a second roadblock. As the soldier stuck the point of his rifle into the car this time, Alison said firmly, 'We are getting out of this tin-pot dictatorship and we are not coming back.' After negotiating our way out of the roadblock in much the same way as we had done the first, we left Lesotho the next day.

13

BLACKENED MAN

WE CALL THE MINERS OF COAL, GOLD AND DIAMONDS!
Let us speak of the dark shafts and the cold compounds
far from our families.

(South African Congress Alliance summons
to draw up the Freedom Charter)

It was difficult turning our back on all that human need. It still is difficult. However, the debacle of our visit to Lesotho confirmed that we were not cast in the same mould as the thousands of intrepid missionaries who risked all, their families included, to bring Christianity to Africa. Alison sensibly pointed out that if I wanted to be a David Livingstone, I should leave my family behind in England, as Livingstone was forced to do after taking his wife and three children on a missionary expedition into the African interior that nearly killed them all. I hoped she did not mean it. Neither of us could avoid a sense of failure.

Back in Oxford, with my dream of returning to Lesotho in tatters, I rather self-pityingly thought my life's work had come to an end. There was nothing that I particularly wanted to do in England. Up till then it had provided a sanctuary to begin our family in relative safety and an opportunity to test my vocation to the church. I had always assumed that sooner or later there would be a call back to Southern Africa and that we would return. After all the emotional turmoil of the abortive visit, I resigned myself to the thought that I was now part of the South African diaspora, that people in Britain, Europe, North America and Australia, who put a brave face on things but are always silently hoping and praying for a tomorrow in Cape Town, Johannesburg, Durban, or one of the smaller towns and villages of the beloved country.

I despondently explored several different possibilities and nearly settled to be a country parson on the Kentish Downs. What stopped me in the end was a sense that I was not called, as George Orwell put it, 'to preach upon eternal doom and watch my walnuts grow'. But what was there to do in this cold climate? Further enquiries and job applications then led to an opportunity to combine my interest in business ethics with a student ministry in the University of Durham. I was offered the post of Solway Fellow and Chaplain at University College, and asked to start at the beginning of the new academic year in October 1992. Alison agreed to move to what southerners, such as herself, regard as the arctic North East of England after I described our new home. It was to be a second-floor college apartment in Cosin's Hall, an imposing seventeenth-century building on Palace Green, between the majestic Norman cathedral and castle, a World Heritage Site.

As soon as we had settled into our magical new home, I set out to explore the building consistently voted the most beautiful in Britain, Durham Cathedral. At the east end, near the great rose window, lies the shrine of Cuthbert, the saintly hermit of the Farne Islands, who was loved by seals and birds as well as by man. In the choir is the imposing seat of the once mighty Prince Bishops of Durham, who reigned over a vast palatinate with its own standing army and who, in the Middle Ages, were charged with the task of keeping out the Scots. At the western end of the cool and vaulted interior is the Galilee Chapel, with the tomb of the Venerable Bede, the author of the first history of the English nation. It was in this chapel, at the end of my tour, that I came across an exhibition displaying the work of the Lesotho and Durham Diocesan Link. The photographic display of BaSotho, dressed in their colourful blankets in the Maluti Mountains, where we had been only a few months before, ended with an invitation to support the work of the Link. Whether or not it was a coincidence or a strange providence that had brought us to Durham, I left the cathedral with a lightness in my step. Here was a place to be. Here was work to do.

With the Lesotho and Durham Link providing me with a link with Africa, our seven years at the centre of an academic community were to be happy and stimulating ones. Together we tried to engage with the University of Durham at a number of levels. Alison became even more involved with students than me in her work at the University Health Centre. After a while I discovered that she was fielding many of the students for whom I was paid to provide pastoral support. She sang in the University of Durham Choral Society, which held concerts in the unsurpassable setting of Durham Cathedral. Despite my best efforts to persuade her not to, because I thought she was only doing it for my sake, she worked three sessions a week in the high security Frankland Prison. For a time she was doctor to the mass murderer Dr Harold Shipman.

I was fortunate to have in Durham Castle two chapels, which encouraged the use of a variety of styles of worship. The Tunstal Chapel, dating from the Reformation, with its fine organ and choir, provided the perfect setting for choral evensong. As a contrast, the intimate Norman chapel, in the bowels of the castle, provided an atmospheric setting for the more contemporary Iona Community liturgy. I was also fortunate to have the support of Christian academics who contributed to the preaching in the two chapels and opened our eyes and ears to a variety of subjects ranging from the beauty of the English hymn to the complexity of the non-realist theology of the Sea of Faith Movement. Perhaps the most memorable sermon series of all was the one given by the

University Orator and Professor of English, David Fuller, who recited extracts from the sermons of John Donne to a packed chapel once a week over a full term.

Three of the chapel sermon series were so outstanding that I edited them and had them published. *Veritatis Splendor: a Response*, a collection of Anglican responses to the Pope's encyclical on moral theology, with a foreword by the Archbishop of York, John Habgood, made it into the *Church Times* top ten religious books of the year. The book was widely reviewed, even in the Vatican. From there the leading Catholic moral theologian, Bernard Häring, wrote appreciatively in the *Tablet* that 'seldom have I read a book with such burning interest. This small volume of 120 pages, a series of addresses given to Durham University, is in my opinion a significant event.' He contrasted it with the unbending moral teaching of the Pope's encyclical, which he admitted had caused him long lasting seizures of the brain when he first read it, and went on to conclude that 'it is urgent that a continuing conversation should be sustained between the two Communions, not only for the sake of a deeper unity, but in the hope of their being enabled to bring from their shared experience and resources a more intense light to bear upon the moral perplexities of humankind'.

My least effective time as Chaplain was spent in the college bar after 11 p.m., when the normally delightful student company became a trifle incoherent and boisterous. I learned that this was the witching hour when the college chaplain risked being ambushed by pretend atheists, anarchists and sexual deviants of every kind. They thought me so shockable. I put it down to my dog collar, that badge of the innocent cleric, which they could still just make out with their blurring vision. My students did me so much good. They made me feel so young. I would have happily remained a college chaplain for the rest of my life, and at times resented the academic half of my job, that of Solway Fellow, for progressively distancing me from students by requiring me to complete that academic rite of passage, a doctorate.

Rather than research some distant figure or treatise from the past, and risk ending up knowing a lot about a very little, I decided to take the opportunity of my fellowship to try to better understand the society I now found myself to be a part of. I was particularly interested by the political, social and economic revolution of the 1980s associated with the first and only British woman Prime Minister, Margaret Thatcher. This was just really getting underway when I started reading theology at Oxford in 1983, and while I had followed the ensuing debate from a distance, I never really had the time to fully engage with it. However, I was aware that Thatcherism not only flew in the face of the Christian socialism I had up until then uncritically accepted but was also widely held to deny the Church of England's social teaching. What made it all the more intriguing was that, from the little I knew of the 1970s in Britain, it was difficult to dismiss the nagging thought that the country and the economy was in need of a little of the lady's hand-bagging.

I ended up by focusing my research on the most provocative part of Thatcherism, the sale or privatisation of the nationalised industries. This sale of 'the family silver', as the former Conservative Prime Minister Harold Macmillan described it, not only resulted in some very fat cats but also ended the mix of public and private ownership of economic enterprise, which some held to have headed off a communist revolution in Britain after the Second World War. The policy was certainly a frontal attack on the trade union movement, which regarded the former public corporations as their power base. For them, privatisation meant an empowering of the capitalists at the expense of the workers and, once again under the whip of private sector managers, they feared a reversal of the steady gains in pay and conditions they had achieved over more than a century of the democratic labour movement. While some of the firebrands talked of a counter-revolution, having alienated most of the country in the 'Winter of

Discontent' of 1979, when they recklessly turned on the Labour government of Jim Callaghan and gave Margaret Thatcher her opportunity, they were forced to settle for a costly boycott of privatisation share issues.

Another reason for choosing privatisation was that it was a burning issue in the staunch Labour Party stronghold of Durham. The resentment of Margaret Thatcher's rout of the National Union of Mineworkers in 1986, which created the conditions for the successful implementation of privatisation, was all too apparent at the annual Durham Miners' Gala. This took place on Durham racecourse, a wide, open space in the city by the River Wear. It started with the arrival of the colliery bands, with their stirring tunes and colourful banners, representing mining communities all over County Durham. It was often a highly charged occasion and, at the Gala held during the General Strike of 1926, the Dean of Durham Cathedral narrowly escaped being thrown into the River Wear after he was mistaken for the unpopular Bishop of Durham, Hensley Henson, who had publicly denounced the strikers.

The first year I attended the Gala, the controversial Labour minister and Christian socialist Tony Benn was the guest speaker. After a rousing address, the whole gathering moved from the racecourse to the cathedral to celebrate the Christian foundations of Britain's Labour movement and to lay wreaths at the monument to miners who had lost their lives in mining accidents. Arthur Scargill, or, as he was affectionately known to his supporters, 'King Arthur', the President of the National Union of Miners, read the lesson. It was in the hymn singing that the depth of the Christian influence on this community struck me most because there was no need of hymn sheets, the congregation knew the words by heart. The event reminded me of the Blackened Man of the early eighteenth century, a miner whose body had been tarred after his execution, and then hung on a gibbet on the Jarrow marshes, as a terrible example of what happens when workers challenge the power of capital.

My third main reason for choosing to study privatisation was that it directly challenged the aspirations of the African National Congress, which had pledged, in the Freedom Charter, the authoritative statement of the aims of the liberation movement drawn up in 1955, to transfer South Africa's mines, banks and public utilities to common ownership. It was as ambitious a programme of nationalisation as that of Britain's Atlee administration after the Second World War and, having provided the perfect excuse to ban the ANC as an organisation bent on imposing Communism when it was announced in 1955, I feared that any attempt to implement the programme in a post-apartheid situation might lead to South Africa being punished again by the international community, by the withholding of much-needed investment. Furthermore, as Britain's experiment with nationalised industry was not an entirely happy one, I hoped to learn from what went wrong, with a view to contributing to the expected future debate about the direction of a post-apartheid economy.

As a student of management, privatisation also marked for me a disappointing end to the experiment with the organisational model chosen for the nationalised industries of an independent public corporation, at arm's length from government. Like many at the time, I had high hopes that this type of corporation, by fixing the profit motive within the wider framework of public service, was the answer to the destructive conflictual relationship between capital and labour, which has plagued industrial society at the cost of millions of lives in the ideological clashes of the nineteenth and twentieth centuries. I also favoured the model because it represented something of a synthesis of the socialist model of a corporation owned by its workers and the rival capitalist model of a limited liability company owned by private shareholders. Given the relatively short time which the experiment had run, and the frequent political interventions, which meant that it had hardly been given a chance, I was keen to form an opinion as to whether the public corporation really was the failure it was judged to be.

By the time I completed my research, however, the Thatcher revolution had gone global and, like a tsunami, has swept all before it. In the context of deregulated capital markets, there appeared to be no alternative to privatisation if a country wanted to attract investment for growth, increased prosperity, more jobs and the renewal of public services. It was a case of, to borrow some words from Bishop Hensley Henson, 'the economic framework leaves little freedom to the moralist, *necessitas non habet legem*. Even the British Labour Party was forced to abandon its famous Clause IV commitment to public ownership.

Back in the new South Africa, as I have recounted, Nelson Mandela's ANC responded to these developments by quietly shelving the nationalisations promised in the Freedom Charter. In the hope of attracting foreign investment, the new government adopted the conservative macro-economic policies advocated by the IMF and World Bank and, fearful of provoking its trade union allies, embarked on a cautious programme of privatisation. While the austerity measures earned the respect of financial markets, they cost the poorest people jobs, wage cuts and rising utility bills. Many simply could not pay and had their services disconnected, something that was rarely done under apartheid. And still they await the rush of new investment that is promised to transform their lives.

While I was forced to accept that there was little hope of reversing Thatcherism, I tried to salvage something from my research by exploring the outlines of an alternative political project, which I hoped might inform my choices as a citizen in the decidedly bleak world brought about by her global revolution. I ended up by identifying five main points, which I still think stand the test of time.

The first is that political, economic and social revolutions are best avoided. In addition to the millions of victims piled up on the ideological pyres of the twentieth century, I drew in support on the wisdom of the revered Anglican Archbishop

William Temple, who, although he died before the war ended, lived just long enough to make a critical contribution to the thinking behind the reconstruction of British society after the Second World War. He advocated a middle way between the Christian socialism of radicals, such as the economic historian R.H. Tawney, and the economic liberalism of conservatives, such as Bishop Hensley Henson. What he urged was gradual, incremental reforms to the existing system, or, 'transformation by adaptation, not by destruction'.

I also drew on an early disciple of Margaret Thatcher, who later turned one of her fiercest critics, John Gray, then Professor of Politics at Oxford University. His main charge against her was that she failed to recognise, along with all the Enlightenment thinkers, with their rival secular versions of a world transformed, that political life 'is an almost desperately humble task of endless improvisation'. It is the kind of simple wisdom frustrated rail commuters and the surviving victims of recent rail disasters have been shouting at politicians ever since the privatisation of British Rail. If this more modest assessment of all politics can offer is accepted, then we should be more supportive of the politician who shuns the grand vision and is content to plug away at delivering modest but sustainable improvements.

On the basis of this gradualist approach, I set out a programme of organic political reform, starting with democracy itself. In the light of the failures of both statist solutions, such as nationalisation, which have sought to promote social justice by expanding the state, and *laissez-faire* solutions, such as privatisation, which have sought to shrink the state, I opted for the *Third Way* social philosophy championed by Anthony Giddens, the former Director of the London School of Economics. This puts its hope in the renewal of civil society, encouraged by a raft of measures which tries to enable an active citizenry, on the one hand, to insist on responsive, transparent and accountable government from large political bureaucracies and, on the other, to challenge concentrations of property-based power. Importantly, it recognises that free citizens deserve to some extent the government they get and the fat cats they allow.

My experience as an activist in South Africa also prodded me in this direction. In the apartheid era the extra-parliamentary political, religious, civic, academic, cultural, sporting and family associations, like a swarm of bees, kept harrying and stinging the racist parliamentary political parties. Their heroic resistance demonstrated for me the power of an active citizenry. And their vigilance did not stop with the toppling of apartheid. Since then each citizen has been exhorted to take personal responsibility for what is known in the new South Africa as *masekane*, or democratic nation-building. This mobilisation of 'the people' has not been comfortable for the ruling ANC, which has, for instance, found its complacency on AIDS challenged by groups campaigning for the free distribution of antiretroviral drugs. Civil society has also proved itself indispensable by challenging corruption in government and in the private sector, and by protesting the growing inequality produced by economic policies which favour the new Black middle class.

Having started with freedom, I turned my attention next to the more contentious value of equality by exploring the thorny issue of redistributing income and wealth. In addition to the wide and widening disparity in income and wealth in Britain between the South and the North, this part of my new project was suggested by the challenges that a post-apartheid South Africa faced, with its very unequal distribution of income and wealth (especially land). And, as anyone who has played the game of Monopoly knows, without some kind of Jubilee – the ancient Jewish law whereby debts were cancelled and property returned to its original owner every forty-nine years – the operation of the free market ends with one person owning the whole board.

The British debate on this issue was interesting because something of a consensus had emerged by the 1990s, which held that the already redistributive taxation system had reached a ceiling; it was thought counter-productive to soak the rich any more because they simply took their wealth and put it in a tax haven somewhere else. Certainly the experience of a wealth tax in Scandinavia, some continental European countries and Ireland has been mixed. So better leave income tax rates where Mrs Thatcher had lowered them, even though inequality was rising for the first time in decades, and stick with the existing inheritance tax, which was gradually turning the great piles of the feudal aristocracy into weekend theme parks for the public and tourists. It followed that, if one accepted a cap on public revenue, the only way to improve the lot of the man or woman in the street was to make each pound stretch a bit longer. This meant a fresh look at public services to see whether they were providing value for money. As a result the reform of public services, in particular the National Health Service and education, has dominated British politics in recent years.

My experience as a British parent, however, would not allow me to accept this approach to taxation. In comparison with the magnificent schools I attended, I could not but be struck by the decrepit buildings and inadequate playing fields of the state schools attended by my children. The Durham Johnston School, one of the best-performing comprehensive schools in the country, was still using Portakabins 'temporarily' installed as classrooms over thirty years ago. Apart from a football pitch, its other sporting facilities were so ancient as to be virtually unusable. The state of the school fully supported the warnings of the columnist Will Hutton, who, at the time, took every possible opportunity to point out that unless Britain invested in its human capital, the source of wealth in a post-industrial society, she could not expect to maintain her widely envied political, social and economic achievements.

As the spouse of a doctor I was also aware of just how run-down the NHS had become. While doubtless there was considerable waste and inefficiency, the dilapidated plant, low pay and even lower morale suggested that the scope of reform was limited without a massive programme of capital investment. It looked to me from my African perspective that the then current British political generation was shamefully neglecting the remarkable post-war achievement of the Welfare State, which it had inherited as a trust and should be handing on in good shape to the next generation. I concluded that the reform of public services justified a wealth tax.

As the third part of my alternative project, I addressed the challenges posed by the large business corporations, which dominate the British and global economy. Here I wanted to recapture the medieval sense in which a corporation is first and foremost a human community, whose members freely choose to promote the common good together because they can achieve more than by acting alone. This ideal appears to have been largely lost sight of in modern Anglo-Saxon capitalism, when the commercial purposes of the corporation – the pursuit of profit and the sharing of risk – have taken on such over-riding importance that they have produced massive, imper-sonal bureaucracies, which stifle the individual, eliminate competition and undermine democracy. Corporations of this type are Leviathans. They eat people or oppress them and make them very sick.

As a way of recovering the medieval ideal of a corporation, I supported the modest reform proposed and championed by, among others, Professor John Kay, the first Director of the Saïd Business School. This calls for the legal status of management as the agent of the shareholders to be changed to that of trustee of the corporation as a whole, thereby placing on management the responsibility of maintaining and enhancing the value of all the assets of the corporation, including those intangible ones, such as its relationship with local communities. The change also recognises that employees, suppliers, local communities and future generations all have an interest or stake in the corporation – often a much bigger stake than its shareholders.

Somewhat predictably, this reform is bitterly opposed by shareholders on the ground that it would take management's 'eye off the ball'; instead of concentrating on making profits for investors, they would run about like politicians desperately trying to satisfy an impossible number of conflicting stakeholder demands. There may be some truth in this. However, the fear is probably exaggerated because no corporation can afford to ignore investors, and must, if it is to survive, take into account the long-term interests of all its stakeholders. As John Kay has pointed out, the senior management of a large corporation behaves like a board of trustees most of the time. But they need to be legally recognised as trustees for those few, critical choices, when they are compelled by their fiduciary duty to put the short-term interests of shareholders before the interests of the corporation as a whole.

As the fourth and final part of my alternative project, I turned my attention from the individual corporate players to the game itself, the modern global market. Here it is worth recalling that, not so very long ago, the market was a simple mechanism for dealing with the economic surpluses of a subsistence economy; what you did not eat you bartered. The next stage was a limited division of labour and specialisation producing small market towns. Even as late as the Middle Ages the market was still a very minor part of human existence. For this reason, as the doyen of economic historians John Kenneth Galbraith has pointed out, 'Economics as we know it did not exist.' But all this changed with the Industrial Revolution and, more recently, the revolution brought about by computers. Since then, the volume, value and complexity of market transactions have grown on a staggering scale. Now human life without the market is unthinkable. We can wake up in London on a cold winter's day and can enjoy fresh fruit and roses cut the previous day in the Cape. More importantly, peasants in China, India and Mozambique can begin to climb out of poverty.

Frighteningly, though, at the same time as the global market has become essential for human flourishing, its development, like the internet, threatens to outstrip our ability to control it. The ball has started to whiz about so fast that the rules of the game and the referee find it difficult if not impossible to keep up. This is especially the case in the capital and money markets, which account for most of the billions of daily market transactions. The result is that many of those who would like to play have been forced on to the sidelines, to watch others play for their property and resources and, sometimes, their whole countries. Great Britain herself, with the fourth largest economy in the world, has not escaped unscathed. Not even that thoroughbred of British banks Warburgs has been able to withstand the spate of foreign takeovers of the once proud independent City financial institutions. And the former giant conglomerate ICI, once the bellwether of British manufacturing on Teeside, is now largely owned by companies headquartered abroad.

In this increasingly anarchic and violent game, without radically changing the rules, there is no alternative but to strengthen the power of the referee. This must involve increasing the powers of regulators and sharing more of the power of national governments with larger regional democratic assemblies, such as the European Union and the emerging African Union, and international institutions, such as the United Nations – even at the cost of a loss of national sovereignty and increased red tape and corruption. These lesser costs simply have to be borne because otherwise the unfettered forces of the market will succeed in dividing the world into two camps, the few who own most of its assets and the many who are little better off than wage slaves – the classical conditions for violent revolution and civil war. Add the frustration of privatised local resources, such as a water supply, owned by a remote foreign company perceived to be charging exorbitant rates, and such a future cannot but be explosive. The ritual mob violence on May Day in London will look like a firecracker.

With all the signs pointing in the direction of increasingly violent resistance against global capitalism, I concluded that it was now a matter of human survival that we should gain control over the market forces which threaten to plunge the world back into a Hobbesian state of nature, where every man has a right to every other, even to their bodies. When my fixed-term appointment in the University of Durham drew to a close at the end of the academic year in 1999, I therefore decided to try to actively support those working to introduce reforms along the lines outlined in my alternative political project. As we each need to focus our finite energies on limited and achievable aims, I chose to concentrate mine on the movement for corporate social responsibility, which, together with enlightened business leaders and a wide array of civil society groups, and from mass protests at the World Economic Forum to individual consumer decisions to buy fair trade coffee, is trying to tame Leviathan.

Like the fictitious Precious Ramotswe, who set up her No. 1 Ladies Detective Agency in Botswana, I set up my office and hung my sign outside sheepishly thinking that no one would ever hire my services. Not having a high street location in Gaberone, I developed a website to advertise my programmes and sent out a few letters. While waiting for a response, I taught business ethics at the University of Durham Business School and at Henley Management College. To my surprise, my first corporate client was South African Breweries, then emerging as a global brewer concerned to maintain its reputation as a good corporate citizen in the emerging markets of Eastern Europe and China. British American Tobacco was next with what Bishop David Jenkins, who helped me facilitate a stakeholder dialogue as part of a corporate social and environmental report, called its 'search for an impossible repentance'. Then the second largest bank in the world, HSBC, asked me to produce a film on terrorist finance and money-laundering prevention. It was while working on this film that I made the discovery that my own story is part of a much, much bigger story.

14

IMPERIAL TERROR

When I see Colonel Joll again, when he has the leisure, I bring the
conversation around to torture. 'What if your prisoner is telling the
truth,' I ask, 'yet finds he is not believed? Is that not a terrible
position? Imagine: to be prepared to yield, to yield, to have nothing
more to yield, to be broken, yet to be pressed to yield more! And
what a responsibility for the interrogator! How do you ever know
when a man has told you the truth?'

(J.M. Coetzee, *Waiting for the Barbarians*)

The United States used to hold little interest for me. I considered the distance, both geographical and cultural, from
Teyateyaneng to London quite enough for one lifetime and so
had little incentive to explore how people lived on the other
side of the Atlantic. Besides, I suspected that the USA and SA
would have a lot in common; they were, after all, both former
British colonies, spoke variants of the Queen's English and even
shared similar race problems. Given this shared history and my
upbringing in the colonies, I also found that I could not work
myself up to share the British resentment of American
penetration of their old world. I found the American conquest
of the City of London, with its ruthlessly smug 'gentlemanly
capitalism', for instance, rather satisfying; at least it meant there
could be no confusion that capitalism is red in tooth and claw.

Alison, by contrast, presents a reliable barometer of English disdain for all things American. She hates the banality of Hollywood films, and fears for the day when the BBC will lose its licence and go the way of American television and radio, with their endless commercials. She is deeply scornful of their private health care system, with its parasitic insurance industry encouraging expensive medicine and threatening to export a litigious culture to Britain. She was especially incensed when their money seemed to be taking over what she considered England's finest achievement, the University of Oxford; not even Balliol is safe, she would say, after the American scientist and Nobel Laureate Baruch Samuel Blumberg took over from Anthony Kenny as Master, and a young American clergyman, with seemingly little more to commend him than an attractive southern drawl, replaced my chaplain and tutor, Peter Hinchliff, when he was appointed Professor of Ecclesiastical History. While all this passion never failed to amuse me, it did not cause me to take sides: I neither hated nor loved the United States of America – it was simply there – a not particularly interesting colossus on the other side of the water.

All this changed for me on 9/11. The shock of watching on television the Twin Towers fall, followed by scenes of rejoicing in the Middle East and in parts of Africa, forced me to revise my personal map of the world. The United States of America was clearly the Rome of our day. The attack also challenged me to explore why young Arabs had developed such an intense hatred for America that they were prepared to sacrifice themselves in such an undeniably audacious raid. It certainly put into the shade the increasingly violent anti-capitalist protests of Western civil society at Seattle, Prague and Genoa. Here was resistance of an altogether different order, promising an altogether different civilisation based on the Muslim understanding of community, the Umma. What was one to make of it?

My commission to produce a film on terrorist finance and

money-laundering prevention provided an opportunity to explore this question because it was to take me to America, where I could observe for myself the object of so much anger. It also opened a door for me into the dark and cavernous world of money-laundering. Technically this activity involves criminals placing the proceeds of crime into the financial system, disguising where the money came from, making it impossible to trace by layering it through multiple bank accounts and financial instruments and, finally, investing it in some secure nest egg. Because money-laundering makes crime pay, it is the mother of all crime.

I had been aware of money-laundering as an issue for some time because civil society organisations, such as Transparency International, had protested against British banking complicity in the Sani Abacha scandal of the early 1990s. The banks were accused of helping the Nigerian dictator launder some 4 billion pounds of his country's oil wealth. The money, which should have gone to pay for improved health care, education, roads and other development infrastructure, was siphoned off to secure a comfortable retirement abroad for him and his large family. The banks protested their innocence, but as one money-laundering expert confided in me, all banks competed for the dirty money of the likes of Sani Abacha because it was highly profitable and perfectly legal to do so; such a wealthy customer was even assigned a personal bank manager.

The government bowed to pressure, ordered an investigation and promised a report. Sani Abacha then ensured the scandal would run and run by committing the heinous crime of ordering the trial and execution in 1995 of the human rights activist Ken Saro-Wiwa, and eight other Ogoni people, who claimed that they had been framed for their opposition to the operations of the oil company Shell in the Niger delta.

Meanwhile, the United States was facing a worsening drugs problem. In response to high levels of drug addiction and the attendant violent crime, fuelled by the ease with which international drug cartels were able to launder money through the American banking system, the United States passed a series of anti-money-laundering laws. It also sponsored the Financial Action Task Force, an international initiative to try to combat money-laundering worldwide by having all countries adopt the same or similar legislation. With the Sani Abacha scandal festering in the background and civil society organisations agitating for a change in the law, Britain signed up to the initiative and introduced its own law against money-laundering.

Then came the attack on the Twin Towers and the Pentagon. The devastation and the threat of further terror focused attention on money-laundering as never before. It was suddenly realised that a sophisticated modern terrorist network such as al Qaida was capable of using the international financial system to fund individual acts of terror anywhere in the world. A hunt for terrorist finance ensued in all Western financial capitals. In the City of London, the newly formed Financial Services Authority threatened draconian fines for any financial institution, not only caught laundering dirty money, but also failing to introduce adequate anti-money-laundering controls and training for staff. Considering what had gone on before, this represented a sea change in attitude among financial professionals to behaviour they had, only a few years before, regarded as an unavoidable part of their business.

My commission to produce a film was part of this seismic shift in corporate social responsibility within the financial services industry. After it was finished, I was invited by the Head of Global Anti-Money Laundering at Citigroup, the world's largest bank, to show it at the American Bankers Association conference held in Washington, DC in 2003, and took the opportunity to make a tour of the eastern seaboard of the United States. Needless to say, I discovered a country of sharp contrasts, which confirmed something of both Alison's and my prejudices, but also challenged them. It was certainly a more culturally mixed and therefore more interesting society than I had envisaged.

The Washington conference fairly bristled with frightened people, many of whom worked in vulnerable high-rise office blocks like the Twin Towers. The most important point I came away with was the impossibility of guaranteeing safety against terrorist attack. This uncomfortable reality was impressed on all when the Deputy Head of the newly created Department of Homeland Security, one of the speakers, was forced to admit being embarrassed by a young college student who, the previous week, had hidden knives, similar to those used by the 9/11 terrorists, on board several American aeroplanes and then had reported the breaches of security to the police. Instead of trying a similar stunt, the government minister asked delegates to send their complaints about security failures directly to him.

I arrived back in London from the conference to hear a senior British intelligence officer reiterate her warning that a terrorist attack on London, possibly using weapons of mass destruction, was 'inevitable'. With all I had learned in Washington, this filled me with the foreboding that we have all been sleepwalking into what may yet become a cataclysmic conflict. With that unsuspecting generation of Europeans who allowed their young men to stumble into the trenches of the First World War in mind, I silently resolved to pack our two teenage children off to live with their grandparents in South Africa if the terrorists succeeded in bringing their campaign to the streets of Britain. I also decided that I urgently needed to find out more about the Arabs.

My only visit to the Middle East was to the Holy Land, shortly before I was ordained a priest in 1988. Like so many who visit only for the religious sites of two millennia ago, the plight of the Palestinian people mostly passed me by. At the time, it was as if they had been successfully rubbed out of the story, so much so that Alison and I were able to combine a pilgrimage with a very restful holiday at the Scottish Episcopal Hospice in Tiberias, on the shore of the Sea of Galilea. My happiest memory is of sitting, with a gin and tonic, in a deckchair on the balcony of our room and looking out on the peaceful lake. Recalling this memory, I asked myself why it was that, notwithstanding their ancient and moral right to live in Palestine, I had uncritically accepted the Jews' right to a state of Israel, when the Palestinians clearly have a prior right to the country. I was forced to admit that, with my Western eyes, the Palestinians were largely invisible to me. As a veteran of the anti-apartheid struggle in South Africa, I should have known better.

In order to explore more of the reasons for my partial sightedness, I started by putting aside the rosy picture of empire I had from my grandparents' MBE and OBE. In my mind's eye, I left their home in Teyateyaneng, with its silver tea set and Worcester china, and walked over the road to the local recruiting centre for the mines, with its long queue of BaSotho waiting to be taken on and sent off to Igoli. Still in my imagination, I boarded the train to Johannesburg with them, from where I took a taxi to the fine Anglo American head office building in the city centre. There I pictured myself meeting Cecil John Rhodes just after the Boer War, and listening to his noble ideas about how he was going to use his wealth to make Africans, from the Cape to Cairo, into little Englishmen. Still in my imagination, I then sailed on the next ship bound for London, where I went straight to the biggest bank in the world and was received by the most powerful man in the world, Baron Rothschild, Rhodes's financier.

There I paused to try to make sense of what I knew about the White Man's contribution to South Africa. Without the capital the Rothschild Bank controlled and provided, I accepted that it would have been impossible for the Bantu to have made the transition from their cattle-based economy to the strongest modern economy in Africa. Rhodes and Rothschild therefore helped bring South Africa into the modern world. Nevertheless, I could not put out of my mind the human cost of those forced to take the train to

Johannesburg and, in recent decades, that horribly infectious and deadly sickness they take home. Neither could I excuse the failure to ensure that some part of their gold, diamonds and platinum should be turned into jewellery in Africa, where it could have provided good employment for thousands and allowed Africans to express themselves in the fine art they once produced and traded in the great cities of Timbuktu and Kano. I concluded that behind the fine façade projected by British imperialists there was a very different reality.

From these reflections on how the British Empire worked in Africa, I now better understood the two-faced nature of Western imperialism, which masks its will to power in the guise of championing individual freedoms and civilisation. I also realised that, while imperialists can co-opt domestic and imperial elites by projecting a culture of virtue, they cannot blunt the reality for the excluded majority. For them, empire is a monopoly on the use of violence achieved by superior economic and military power for the exploitation of their natural resources. And because virtue and violence do not stand prettily together, imperialists have to render invisible the excluded majority by reducing them in some way, so that they can be looked over and not be seen; hence Rudyard Kipling's description of the Indian as 'half devil and half child'; the South African humiliation of a manservant by calling him 'boy'; and the Israeli description of the Arabs as fit only for carrying water and hewing wood.

Relating all this to the American-led 'war on terror', it was clear that Western imperialists delude themselves when they think they can pass themselves off as liberators. In any case, the picture of the fuel-guzzling sports utility vehicles of America is now so fixed in the global consciousness, that it is impossible for the United States to conceal the true motive for its presence in a select number of energy-rich countries. Indeed, one only need think of gold and black gold (oil) to appreciate that Western involvement in the Middle East and in Southern Africa is part of the same story of the Western struggle for global supremacy, which has involved international piracy practised on a grand scale.

Here it is worth recalling how the British Empire was started in the sixteenth century by English pirates preying on the already well-established naval empires of the Spanish and Portuguese. After English adventurers, such as Walter Raleigh, had failed to find any gold and silver in the New World themselves, they did the next best thing by attacking the Spanish fleet in the hope of finding ships laden with treasure. When the Spanish retaliated by sending their doomed Armada against England, Queen Elizabeth I launched a foreign policy that set out to found British colonies as strategic bases for commanding the high seas. In the course of the next three centuries, by going to foreign countries and making off with their wealth, Britain was to create the greatest empire the world has ever seen.

If there is any doubting the essentially piratical nature of this empire, one need only note to what lengths Britain, the land of the free, was prepared to go in search of booty. After Spanish gold and silver, the next most lucrative trade was in sugar. This took Britain into the Caribbean and, in order to secure sufficient labour for the sugar plantations, into the trans-Atlantic slave trade. From the Caribbean it was a short jump into North America for tobacco and cotton, which required still more slaves. The trade in tea and spices led into India, and the subjugation of the ancient and prosperous Indian civilisation. In search of more tea, the British then foisted a drug culture on the Chinese. Little interest was shown in Southern Africa until the sea route around the Cape had to be secured against Napoleon by the seizure of the Cape from the Dutch in 1795. It was then only the discovery of diamonds and gold in the two Boer republics of the Orange Free State and Transvaal, which moved Britain to conquer both the Zulu and the Boers before uniting the whole of South Africa under the Union Jack. Small wonder that the African World Reparations and Repatriation Truth Commission, meeting in Accra in 1999, demanded a staggering £150 trillion from the British as reparation for colonialism and slavery. To this sum, the commission might also have added the cost to Africa of Britain's flourishing arms trade, a calculation that will one day have to be made.

The piracy of the United States, which took over where Britain left off, has been less overt, mainly because it has not had to live beyond its means off a few small islands. Nonetheless, it has been every bit as ruthless in controlling natural resources, such as oil, which it does not have enough of and which it wants to keep from rival hands. In this connection, defenders of empire will point out that wherever there is a deficit of power in the world, one or more empires will rush in to fill the space. This is indisputably true. Indeed, the reality of each of our lives is that they are shaped by one or more of the great empires that rise and fall and compete for mastery over us, and which are so relentless, precisely because they are driven, not only by self-aggrandising ideologues, power-hungry generals, business magnates and idealistic missionaries, but also by the independent decisions of millions of small traders, prospectors, farmers and buccaneers. The gradual control of this army of adventurers over a territory, a country and, finally, a continent takes place by stealth and is totally ruthless because, while individuals may profess the highest principles, the collective will of imperialists brooks no opposition and will kill, maim, imprison and torture any one who gets in the way. Against this broad canvas, one has to accept that the quest for peace, justice and freedom in the world is bound to be elusive and that, while Westerners are not well placed to judge, the best one can say about the empires of Great Britain and the United States is that they may be more humane than their rivals.

However, acknowledging that the Americans may be better rulers than the Ottomans, for instance, cannot excuse the fact that, in the present 'war on terror', the Arabs hold genuine grievances and that their complaints have been ignored by their Western masters for a very long time. Like so many, I learned about this history from the epic film *Lawrence of Arabia*, which presents a telling account of the British betrayal of the Arab nationalist cause. The film reports how T.E. Lawrence was authorised to promise British support for a United Arab Republic stretching from North Africa to Syria in return for Arab military support against the Ottoman Turks, and how, at the end of the war, Britain and France simply replaced the defeated Ottoman Empire in the region by dividing up its former Arab provinces between them as protectorates. They thereby denied Arabs the opportunity of forging a modern secular nation, which might by now have transcended the religious and ethnic divisions of the Middle East and taken its place alongside others in the world as an equal.

Without the unity that is strength, Arab nationalism was then further trampled when Britain and France withdrew after the Second World War, and the United States of America and the Soviet Union stepped in to compete for influence in the region. The year 1958 almost saw a united republic born when the pro-Soviet governments in Syria and Egypt merged to form the United Arab Republic. The Iraqis, after overthrowing their monarchy and establishing a radical republic, were expected to join. But somehow the pro-Western governments in Jordan and Lebanon and Iran held on and the revolution petered out. As it did in Southern Africa, the superpower conflict then turned the whole of the Middle East into a battleground, which claimed many millions of lives in a succession of Arab–Israeli wars and, after the fall of the pro-Western Shah to a Muslim theocracy in Iran, in a prolonged war between Iraq and Iran. With the collapse of the Soviet Union in 1989, the United States was left with the spoils but with very soiled hands.

By the end of the century, with the Muslim theocracy in Iran presenting a radical alternative, the repression of democratic forces, inter-Arab divisions, and the demoralising military defeats at the hand of Israel, left little intact of the once-strong Arab nationalist cause. Without a secular focus for unity, the

Arab resentment of foreign interference and domination turned to that other and always competing focus for unity, Islam, with its ideal of a united Muslim community or Umma. It is this reaction that has now produced the broad-based anti-Western Islamist movement, of which al Qaida is the most ruthless representative.

With this history in mind, it became clear to me why the state of Israel is such a major provocation to the Arabs. Looked at from their perspective, it is simply one more European colony. Once again the British were largely responsible by promising, in the so-called Balfour Declaration of 1917, a homeland for the Jews in Palestine. While the declaration specifically ruled out any diminution of the civil and religious rights of the indigenous Arab and pre-Arab population, whose home Palestine has been for centuries, it did not make clear how the promised Jewish homeland would be achieved without encroaching on the rights of those already there. But at the time no one could have foreseen that the Holocaust would make refugees of the entire Jewish population of Europe, forcing thousands to seek refuge in Palestine.

With the huge influx of European Jews into Palestine during and after the Second World War, the demands of the settler movement for an independent state became unstoppable. In scenes reminiscent of the clashes between European settlers and Zulus in Natal, increasingly violent clashes broke out between Jews and Arabs. On 9 April 1948, only three years after the liberation of Auschwitz, Jewish paramilitaries engaged in what would today be described as the ethnic cleansing of Arab villages, starting with Deir Yassin, just outside Jerusalem and not far from where Yad Vashem, the Holocaust museum, now stands. In the hope that it would save lives, Britain and the United Nations proposed partition of the country and sought to gain Palestinian approval. Britain, under pressure from Jewish terrorists, then ended its mandate, but without having succeeded in getting the Arabs to agree to partition. Although they were still a minority (possibly only a third of the total population), the Jews went ahead and unilaterally declared an independent state of Israel.

The Arab majority understandably opposed Israel's UDI and the partition of their country. They were joined by their fellow Arabs in the first full-scale Arab–Israeli war of 1948, which Palestinians recall as the Nakba or Catastrophe. In the course of this disastrous conflict and the succession of wars that followed in 1956, 1967 and 1973, large numbers of Arabs fled or were expelled from their homes in Palestine to live as refugees in the West Bank and Gaza, in neighbouring Arab states and further abroad. Since the Six-Day War of 1967, with the help of massive American military aid, Israel has occupied the West Bank, Gaza and the Golan Heights. With the construction of its security wall, in defiance of the advisory opinion of the International Court of Justice, the occupation of parts of the West Bank and East Jerusalem looks increasingly permanent.

What is so strikingly familiar to me about the history of the state of Israel is that, as happened in South Africa, the majority of the indigenous population has been disenfranchised, many have been forced from their homes to live in appalling conditions as refugees or exiles, and thousands have been killed. Israel, like South Africa, also openly defies United Nations resolutions and the rulings of the International Court of Justice. With America continuing to provide billions of dollars of military and economic aid to Israel, it is therefore hardly surprising that the two symbols of its global economic and military power, the Pentagon and the Twin Towers, should be marked down by Arab terrorists as legitimate military targets.

After Israel, the invasion and occupation of Iraq is clearly another festering grievance. Here, however, I find myself less sympathetic and must admit to having been surprised by the depth of feeling in Britain against 'Tony Blair's War'. It initially struck me as a clear case of a regime guilty of a gross abuse of human rights that had to be confronted by the international community and, if necessary, ousted by force, even when the risk of intervening and being sucked into a protracted guerrilla struggle was high. In my view, Saddam Hussein had all the makings of a Middle Eastern Hitler: he had fought a prolonged and costly war against Iran; he had used weapons of mass destruction on the Kurds; he had invaded Kuwait; he and his sons were guilty of murderous repression at home; he refused to comply with United Nations weapons inspections; and he was impervious to the suffering inflicted on his people by the economic sanctions imposed by the international community.

Given this long list of indictments, I could not help thinking that those who opposed the war were likely to have no personal experience of living under a vicious tyrannical regime such as that of P.W. Botha, chillingly known as 'The Crocodile', in South Africa and, as a result, failed to grasp what it is like to live in a society where terror can strike at any moment. I was also inclined to support the invasion on the ground that the world will only be a safer place for all its citizens when every would-be Hitler is put on notice that gross abuse of human rights will not be tolerated. Furthermore, I worried that protesters have not grasped the fact of nuclear weapons proliferation in the modern world, and the ease with which chemical and biological weapons of mass destruction can now be manufactured, both of which must justify a pre-emptive strike against a rogue state suspected of preparing to use them. For all these reasons, I concluded that it was one of those wars that *just* had to be fought.

In retrospect, however, it turns out that the suspicion that Iraq was hiding weapons of mass destruction and was prepared to use them was not well founded. Furthermore, while the humanitarian case was clear, the absence of an unambiguous United Nations resolution authorising military intervention undermined the case for war, especially when the dissenting countries were such pillars of the international community as France and Germany. Nevertheless, while I would accept that the invasion may not have been strictly legal under international law, I would not put it on the same moral level as South Africa's illegal occupation of Namibia. But of course it is not what I or any other Western onlooker thinks that is important here. In the context of the struggle for Western supremacy in the Middle East, it was inevitable that the war would attract Arab nationalists and terrorists like a magnet to Iraq and unite them in a war of liberation. Subsequent revelations of the systematic use of torture and sexual abuse of Iraqi prisoners by coalition soldiers can only have confirmed their sense of the righteousness of global jihad.

In the light of this understanding of what is behind the terrorists' hatred of the United States, it is clearly a dangerous folly to think that the 'war on terror' can be won simply by hunting them down. The sense of injustice now runs so deep that any number captured or killed will simply be replaced by new recruits. As the Washington conference impressed on me, it is also a mistake to think that, by raising security to ever higher levels, it is possible to guarantee safety because there are too many breaches in even the most advanced security net. Determined terrorists will always find a way through, as the SWAPO guerrillas did when faced by the forbidding no man's land on the Namibian–Angolan border, which the counter-insurgency unit Koevoet brutally tried to enforce.

There are also unavoidable conflicts of interest between increased security and the values of an open liberal society. The security state can soon become the intrusive surveillance state. In South Africa, BOSS took the excuse of terrorism to ensure that every corner and crevice of society was pried into. Any remotely suspicious person was fair game and public figures posing a threat to the regime were likely to find intimate details of their private lives spread abroad to discredit them. Such a society is one that is always looking over its shoulder. More importantly, it is one where the public debate that is the lifeblood of democracy is stifled and the very voices that might help save lives are not allowed to be heard.

It is also worth drawing attention to what is almost a truism that the terrorists of today will be tomorrow's elder statesmen.

While anyone who points out this irony courts unpopularity in the context of the 'war on terror', it is alarming that so little appears to have been learned about terrorism when terrorists are demonised, their cause judged to be evil, and it is thought that they can be defeated militarily. The apartheid regime made precisely these mistakes by not taking the legitimate grievances of the African people seriously until the whole of Southern Africa had been turned into a war zone. The African National Congress was branded a terrorist organisation, its leaders were accused of being communists and atheists, and its members were ruthlessly hunted down. Nevertheless, the ANC survived, and not only did it survive but its leaders emerged after decades of imprisonment or exile to become the leaders of the new South Africa.

At least both George Bush and Tony Blair have warned that the 'war on terror' will not be over tomorrow or the next day. Indeed, given the intransigence of the main protagonists, we are bound to have more of the same mess for a long while yet. Moreover, with OPEC's share of world oil production set to rise from its present 28 per cent to 40 per cent by 2035, it is more likely than not that the American empire, despite its setbacks in Iraq, will seek to strengthen its grip on the region. There is something of the inevitable, therefore, about the neo-conservative vision of regime change in Syria and Iran as the next step, especially now that the suspected development of a nuclear weapons capability by Iran's theocracy provides the pretext for a pre-emptive strike. The situation is uncannily like that facing Britain at the end of the nineteenth century, when in order to secure its grip on the mineral wealth of Southern Africa, it first had to 'take out' the bellicose Zulu and then engender 'regime change' in the two Boer republics.

The two Western leaders have also been painfully honest that we have entered a new era when the danger of a cata-strophic terrorist attack, the scale of which has not been seen since the atomic bombs dropped on Japan, cannot be ruled out. While this reality sinks in and is perhaps underscored by further carnage in Western capitals, civil society must continue to agitate for both the threat of and the grievances underlying global terrorism to be taken seriously. As the anti-apartheid movement did for South Africa, we must also stand in solidarity with the Palestinian people and Jewish peace activists. Yasser Arafat may not have been a Nelson Mandela, but his courage, the endurance of his people, and the commitment of Jewish and Arab peace campaigners cannot be doubted.

In the mean time, we can hold the new South Africa out as a beacon of hope for the Middle East. While of course there are differences between the two situations, it should not be forgotten just how remote a peaceful settlement in South Africa once looked and how, defying all expectations, the Black majority have forgiven decades of oppression, exploitation and humiliation for the sake of peace. Their former hard-line oppressors have equally unexpectedly come to terms with the *swart gevaar*. Ten years on since the first democratic elections, the minority White population is even discovering distinct advantages in a post-apartheid society, one of which is that young men are no longer conscripted to undergo military service. It is as if the violent prison of apartheid has been lifted for all, demonstrating that no human conflict is utterly without hope of a peaceful resolution and that it is always possible to build more of a rainbow world.

15

FRIENDSHIP CIRCLES

'I trust that, as Ministers of God's Truth and God's message of Love
to mankind, we shall be able before long to meet the Mahomedan
and Brahmin and Buddhist, as well as the untutored savage of South
Africa and the South Pacific, on other and better terms than we do
now – being no longer obliged to maintain every part of the Bible as
an infallible record of past history, and every word as the sacred
utterance of the Spirit of God.'

(John William Colenso)

The miracle of the new South Africa has taught me always to
be hopeful. However, with the geopolitics of the present world
order essentially about oil and with its fault lines lying along
the ancient boundaries of the three great scriptural religions –
Judaism, Christianity and Islam – the rivalry over this scarce
natural resource and religion makes me doubt that there can be
peace in our time. The religious dimension certainly hugely
complicates the 'war on terror' and places a grave responsibility on those of us who are religious to put our houses in
order.

But is it possible for us to do so? Given their violent
proclivities is it perhaps time for us to let go of our mutually
exclusive faiths, especially now that the stakes are so high? In
any case, are they not simply relics of the past with their clergy

ignorant charlatans, peddling dangerous ideas the world would be better without? As a minister of religion myself, who has spent more hours in the House of God than I can count, these questions are unsettling to say the least.

The difficulty we religious face is posed for all to see by Jerusalem, the city of peace. It is anything but peaceful because, as a Western colony in the Middle East and a religious capital of the three Abrahamic faiths, it is where oil and religions meet and clash head on. As such, the city represents something of a rumbling volcano; when dormant, it is the scene of embarrassing petty squabbles between the three religions and between their competing denominations; when it explodes from time to time, it sends its shock waves throughout the world.

At the core of all this instability are the American fundamentalist Christian lobbies. Some measure of their influence on American politics is given by the National Unity Coalition for Israel, an umbrella group for 200 organisations that represents millions of Jews and Zionist Christians. The coalition rejects as anathema any concession by the Israelis that would return land to the Palestinians. Its Christian members are opposed because they believe the creation of the state of Israel and the enlargement of its borders heralds the second coming of Jesus and the great rapture, when they will be taken bodily up into heaven. They also hold the fantastical notion that a Third Temple will be built on the site now occupied by the Dome of the Rock and Al-Aqsa mosque.

On the other side of this fanatical boundary, the minority of Muslim fundamentalists who are suspected of trying to acquire a dirty bomb or some other weapon of mass destruction pose a similar crisis for Islam. It is important to distinguish these extremists from those Muslims who preach and support the enlargement of the Umma, as a response to the imperialism and decadence of the West, but who reject the use of violence. Nevertheless, it is impossible to deny that, wrongly handled, the Koran, like the Bible, has the potential to cause serious violence.

Across the third religious boundary are the Jews for whom a Jewish state is an article of faith. Although the preamble to the Declaration of the State of Israel merely declares that the land of Israel was where the Bible was given to the world, the religious justification of the violence Jews have since resorted to in claiming and holding on to land suggests that many Jews take literally the Biblical belief that God promised the land to the Jews. At least the Jews, unlike the Afrikaner, who made a similar claim in Africa, have faithfully prayed and longed for that tomorrow in Jerusalem. Nevertheless, the notion that God has favourites is no less absurd and self-serving for that.

I shudder to think that there was a time when I was susceptible to similar fundamentalist religious beliefs. In my last year at school, a teacher of religious education invited me to a series of Sunday evening services at the Assemblies of God Church in Pietermaritzburg. It was my first encounter with fundamentalist religion. The hall was packed to hear a visiting speaker deliver a sermon series on 'The End Times'. He was mesmerising and a born orator. I can still remember parts of the sermon, which took the genealogy at the beginning of Matthew's gospel as the basis of a time line leading from Creation to the birth of Jesus. On the basis of the number of generations between these two events, he predicted that the second coming of Jesus was imminent. *Now* was the time for a decision to follow Christ. Any delay and one might be left behind in the great separation of the sheep and the goats. And one would not want to be a goat on that terrible day.

But fear was not the decisive factor in prodding my then nominal Christianity into something more active. The preacher's history of time was far too complicated to take in and, even to my underdeveloped critical faculties, was not very convincing. What did change me were the informal meetings I attended after the service in the home of a couple who were members of the congregation. They were simple, salt of the earth types, and exuded such warmth that the gatherings in their home were infused with a quality of love that I had not encountered before. Here was genuine community. It was on an altogether different plane to the sordid, backbiting school dormitory, which, apart from my family, was the only human community I had known since being packed off to boarding school at age seven. I grabbed at it with both hands.

Mercifully our house church had no interest in revolutionary politics. While I doubt whether any of us were capable of violence, I suspect we might have followed our two leaders into almost anything else. Community was what we were there for. Belief came a long way second. The experience was important for giving me this insight into fundamentalist religion because ever since I have understood that it is pointless trying to combat fundamentalism by intellectual argument – the members of such communities simply shut up their ears. And to some extent it is understandable that they should because the alternative presented by 'respectable' religion often merely offers more of the same backbiting and downright hateful communities they experience in the 'world'.

The first response to the religious fundamentalism that is threatening our post-9/11 world, therefore, has to be the formation of welcoming and supportive human communities, which will draw people away from the violent tendencies in Christianity, Islam and Judaism. Practically, because most people begin to look for authentic community within the religious tradition to which they belong, this challenge will mainly have to be met within our separate religions, where responsible leaders in all three faiths are working hard at providing non-violent communities in their respective churches, mosques and synagogues. However, in the present climate of mistrust, fear and even hatred, it is also important to try to foster altogether new bridging communities, which will unite all people of goodwill in the search for peace.

The difficulties of calling together such inclusive communities are admittedly legion. Nevertheless, anyone with experience of working in community development will know that, even in the most seemingly hopeless situations, fearless and resourceful individuals will emerge and commit themselves to a cause once they can see it is worthwhile. They seem to appear from nowhere, are often the most unlikely people, and are the strongest evidence there is that the human spirit is unquenchable. One such person is the British doctor Elizabeth Carmichael, who, at the height of the township violence, took herself off to South Africa, where she succeeded in breaking through all the barriers apartheid posed to a genuine multiracial community.

I first met Liz at the vigil held on the eve of the second day of my first court martial. She was working at Baragwanath, the massive hospital for Black patients near Soweto, where she tended the injured victims of the township violence and from where she watched Soweto burn on 16 June 1976. Shortly after we met in 1981, after seven exhausting years as a doctor on the front line, she returned to Oxford with her husband, Michael, to write a doctorate on Christian love as friendship. On its completion, at a time when it was not possible for women to be ordained in the Church of England, she went back to Johannesburg to be ordained in the Anglican Church in South Africa. She served on the Wits-Vaal Regional Peace Committee and on the Local Peace Committee in Alexandra, a vibrant historic township, then racked with political violence, in the north-eastern suburbs of Johannesburg. The Queen awarded her the MBE for her peacemaking.

On first meeting Liz, it is difficult to match the Revd Dr and MBE to the slight figure with the cherubic face. But then the eyebrows knit, there is the long pause, eventually the measured sentence, an even longer pause, a second sentence, and that's it. The 'dead air' can be so unnerving that you want to say something, anything, into the silence, before beating a hasty retreat. But, if you hold your nerve, the reward is a shrug, as if to say we should not take ourselves too seriously, a sheepish grin, as if to say we human beings are a daft lot anyway, and a life-long friend. Liz's few honest words and her lived-out understanding of love as friendship made her one of those who kept open channels of communication between the warring communities. This was critically important, especially at those times when the two sides squared up to each other out of fear and ignorance as to what the other was up to, because such people were trusted to listen and help implement sensible proposals to lessen the violence.

Liz's friendship circle, which transcended the racial divide in South Africa, provides me with the basic model for how we ought to go about trying to foster alternative, welcoming and supportive human communities for our post-9/11 world. Like Liz we have to risk not merely dialogue but friendship with people from very different backgrounds to our own. This means that we must forgo the will to power because friendship can only be enjoyed between equals; it can survive vigorous disagreement, disappointment, even betrayal, but at the slightest whiff of imperialism it vanishes. We also need to risk inviting relative strangers into our homes or to our 'local' because talk and food and drink are the basics of community. There we can explore and celebrate our common humanity and commit to those small acts of service which seal the bonds of friendship.

However, if the task of forming new friendship circles or bridging communities is the first step towards building peace in our post-9/11 world, the challenge of engaging with funda-mentalist belief systems cannot be left behind. Two distinct but related tasks present themselves here.

The first is to find appropriate ways of using our treasured and ancient scriptural traditions. As the findings of textual scholars of all faiths have shown, religious language expresses wisdom in myths and metaphor and therefore should not be read as being literally true. It follows that all the great scriptural religions are fallible human traditions carrying the responses of different communities to the mystery of God and to the demands of living together in society. As such, while they provide us with an invaluable pool of wisdom to help us live our lives, because their wisdom relates to situations a long time ago, we should all agree to dip into it carefully, recognising that there are bound to be some jagged rocks lurking below the surface.

The second challenge is posed by our secular traditions, because they can also be accorded the mythical status of an infallible scripture. The wreck of the twentieth century, with its hugely costly wars fought over rival ideologies, is evidence enough of their tendency to encourage violence. However, while secularism has been discredited by its priests, many of our secular traditions have brought huge advances and have helped us better understand our world. The scientific tradition, in particular, has crucially helped us understand the world as a process, which is important from the point of view of accepting that some of the answers we are so desperately searching for have, in a sense, still to emerge. Consequently, there may not be a ready answer to some of the moral dilemmas science faces us with today, and the only way forward is by experimentation, evaluating the results and, depending on whether the human project is advanced or not, deciding whether to continue.

With these insights into the nature of religious and secular truths, our friendship circles should be wary of wasting time on interminable debates, which by their very nature cannot be resolved. These only serve as a diversion from the challenges posed by the violence all around us. Instead, we need to draw on the wisdom of all our religious and secular traditions by asking of each 'truth' what human need it serves, by tolerating differences when different human needs are met, and by gently but firmly discarding those 'truths' which serve no other purpose than to set one lot of people against another. As that early liberal Jesus put this hermeneutic principle: 'the Sabbath was made for man, not man for the Sabbath'.

By calling people out of their existing communities and into new friendship circles, I am not, however, suggesting that we should leave the faith communities to which we belong. No matter how hopeless and thankless a task it sometimes seems, for the sake of peace we must engage with the internal debates of our existing faith communities in order to take responsibility for all that is good in the tradition we have received, and to take it forward in response to new insights into what makes for human flourishing. We also need to prevent the violent fundamentalist beliefs of some of our members from taking over or from becoming so dominant that they distract us from the urgent task of making peace.

It is therefore important to try to keep a foot in both camps. This is bound to be difficult and we must be wary of becoming absorbed in the search for unity at all costs, which goes on in all communities and can perpetuate traditions long past their sell by date; while loyalty is a virtue, it has limits.

In my case, because it threatens to hold the Church of England and the Anglican Communion captive to religious fundamentalism, a critical loyalty means that, along with all fellow Anglicans, I need to engage with the highly charged controversy over homosexuality, which erupted into virtual open warfare following the consecration in the United States of the first openly gay Anglican bishop, Gene Robinson. I do not relish this engagement because, while I value Anglicanism for having provided me with a spiritual and moral framework within which to live my life, and some freedom to explore beyond the frame when it does not appear to be working for me and other people, my church's warring factions have a long history. Indeed, the chief legacy of its highly questionable foundation by Henry VIII and his daughter Elizabeth appears to be a factionalism which renders the Church of England almost incapable of engaging with anything other than itself. As my fellow South African and church historian Peter Hinchliff observed after attending some sessions of the General Synod, the three Anglican factions: catholic, evangelical and liberal, are not only entrenched in their separate positions but hate each other's guts.

As so often happens with one's outlook in general, my attitude towards homosexuality was shaped very early on. It started with my grandmother's tolerant attitude towards a gay couple who were frequent visitors to their home in Basutoland. Henry Smuts, whose accounting firm was based across the border in Bloemfontein, the provincial capital of the Orange Free State, used to audit our family business accounts and would often bring his long-standing partner for the duration of the audit. I recall their visits because, while my grandmother treated them as royally as any of her guests, we were aware as little boys that they were unusual. Henry also made a definite impression as a well-dressed, gentle and cultured man. He was without question a friend of the family.

In the White South Africa of my school and university days, homosexuality was way beyond the pale. I was certainly not aware of a gay South African community, which I suspect was so repressed as to be subterranean. My first encounters with gays therefore had to wait until Stepney, where Bishop Trevor Huddleston was held to have appointed a disproportionate number of gay clergy, apparently because they were the only ones prepared to serve in the difficult inner city parishes of Islington, Hackney and Bow. I was made aware of the pressures they lived under when one, who did his best to conceal his sexual orientation to his congregation under the disguise of a trendy bachelor image, cracked under the strain and was forced to spend a prolonged leave of absence from the parish, some of it in a hospital for the mentally ill. For all of us involved in the denial of his sexuality, it was a lesson about the danger of driving sexuality underground.

Then in 1994 the Turnbull affair triggered an increasingly vicious campaign by conservative evangelicals bent on making homosexuality the litmus test of Christian orthodoxy. The much-loved Bishop of Durham David Jenkins retired and, because some held him to have been too liberal by half, he was replaced by a conservative evangelical, Michael Turnbull, who was thought to be a safe pair of hands. As the Chaplain at Durham Castle, the former main residence of the Prince Bishops of Durham, I had a minor role in the new bishop's enthronement by escorting him on the short walk from the castle over Palace Green to the cathedral. The dignified procession across Palace Green went smoothly until the gay campaigner Peter Tatchell attempted one of his infamous tackles on the bishop, who had publicly expressed his opposition to ordaining openly gay clergy. The awaiting media made much of the incident and with it Michael Turnbull's caution as a young married priest for cottaging. What later struck me was that the ordinary unchurched people of Durham were far more willing to forgive and forget this blip in an otherwise distinguished career than were some of his Christian opponents, such as the Reverend David Holloway, a leader of the conservative evangelical movement Reform, who repeatedly called on Bishop Turnbull to resign.

After the embarrassment of the Turnbull affair, I looked on with dismay at the debacle following Jeffrey John's nomination as Bishop of Reading. It sadly entangled our engaging Welsh archbishop Rowan Williams in a series of damaging compromises, which failed both Jeffrey John, a gay but celibate priest, and the nominating diocesan bishop Richard Harries, the Bishop of Oxford. Given the outstanding record of both men, it was difficult to see the archbishop's failure to back the appointment and the deference he has since shown homophobic Christian leaders, such as the Nigerian Archbishop Peter Akinola, other than as an unseemly failure of nerve and a surrender to the conservatives within the Anglican Communion. In contrast, I could not but admire the leadership given by the Archbishop of Cape Town, Njongonkulu Ndungane, who made it clear that Peter Akinola does not speak for African Christianity, and his predecessor, Desmond Tutu, who publicly declared that the liberation struggle in Southern Africa has led him to the conviction that liberation for Blacks, women and gays are all of a piece.

All the while the controversy in the Anglican Communion had been hotting up, my marriage to Alison has been opening up new perspectives for me on human sexuality. Her medical work has helped me better understand the rainbow world of gender and of sexuality. It seems that at both ends of the spectrum nature and nurture can be very cruel. Alison has found patients who have taken the difficult decision to undergo a sex change particularly distressing. What the prolonged and drastic treatment entailed has alerted me to is that human gender is complex and that, while human sexuality is a different matter, clearly both can be deeply troubled. The lesson for me is that those of us who are happy with who we are should count our blessings and should avoid making those who are unhappy even more miserable.

From my sexual partnership with Alison (and I believe anyone speaking out on either side of this debate should be upfront and personal), I have come to have both a much greater appreciation of the wonder of sex and a respect for what a powerful force it is. Since that picnic we spent together at White Lily in the Natal Drakensberg, her body has become part of my longing. I am a total addict. Marriage has made us 'one flesh' in a deeply satisfying way. Any prolonged bout of abstinence resulting from pressure of work, family and friction between us (and there is plenty of that), not only makes me deeply unhappy but almost incapable of functioning properly. Our 'wild sex' then makes me whole again and sets me free. Sex seems, as if by magic, to be able to restore and renew our friendship. And, very practically, without Alison, I might be a menace in any parish. In the light of these personal observations of how I am, how I work and how I cope, I feel that I must affirm rather than deny the possibility of a life-giving sexual partnership for every person, whatever their sexual orientation.

Finally there is the matter of love. I was never a frontrunner in the marriage stakes. My South African past has left me too guilt-ridden, too self-absorbed and so undomesticated that I entered the starting blocks with a very heavy handicap. That Alison and I have stayed the course thus far has something of the miraculous about it because we have come perilously close to parting company at a number of fences. It also says a lot about Alison, whose capacity to forgive and persevere has been remarkable. But it says most about the sheer grace of love – that sense of belonging, that confidence in the other, that deep-down delight – such that, even when the jump has been totally misjudged and horse and rider are in a tangled mess on the other side, there is only one thing to do, and that is to get up and go on because the thought of life without love is impossible.

Love is also for me an essential refuge from a hostile world. When, as one does, I look back on how little I have achieved, look around and wonder what the point of it all is, and look forward to the inevitable narrowing of possibilities, Alison need only take my hand in hers and all the sense of failure, frustration and fear, which I carry around, melts away. Our little castle is a world replete in itself. We can pull up the drawbridge and, with Alison somewhere in sight, I can be perfectly happy just pottering about. I am ecstatically happy, even perhaps pathetically so, when she leaves off all her busyness and potters with me. Time then stands still. There is no past, no future, only a blissfully absorbing present.

I am not sure whether I could do without sex but I know I could not do without love. Alison's love has taught me to affirm love wherever it is to be found. Furthermore, her love has helped me better understand that profound declaration of John the Evangelist 'God is love', with its attendant warning that to deny love is to deny God.

It follows from all the above that I can find no reason to deny homosexuals the privilege and joy of a loving and sexual relationship. I am therefore in favour of changing the Church of England's rule that requires a homosexual priest to be celibate. I am also happy to bless the marriage of a gay or lesbian couple. Furthermore I look forward to the day when the gay and lesbian Christian community, with its fearless activists, such as Peter Tatchell, are fully welcome in the Church of England and will be set free to give more time to combating other human rights abuses, such as human trafficking, hardcore pornography, paedophilia and casual sex.

On the wider issue of the authority of Biblical texts that condemn homosexuality without qualification or insist on the subordination of women, I simply have to say that they belong to a pre-modern culture, which knew no better. As such, along with all the other unacceptable biblical passages, such as God's command to the Jews, in the Book of Joshua, to ethnically cleanse the local inhabitants of the Promised Land, or the idea of God requiring a human sacrifice of Jesus in order to forgive our sins, we should simply overlook them. Moreover, we should start admitting that we do because otherwise we have nothing to say to the fundamentalists of other religions, who believe that they can draw on their sacred texts to justify all manner of abominations and violence.

As for the strictures of Christian tradition, the glaring failures of church history ought to make us reticent when claiming religious authority for our theological and moral pronouncements. We have, after all, justified slavery and tortured and burnt heretics in the name of Christianity and, once aware of our mistakes, have modified and changed the tradition. One ironic example is the tradition of clerical celibacy, which the newly formed Church of England, with unseemly haste, found good reason to set aside – at least for heterosexual clergy. We can also no longer call on even the best of Christian tradition with the same confidence as we used to because modernity has shown that it is not possible for religious people to assert more than a reverent agnosticism. This modest and understated faith respects, on the one hand, the grounds for atheism and moral scepticism in a scientific understanding of the way the universe is and, on the other, religious experience and the signs of transcendence that support faith in a personal mystery which we call God. While this paradoxical conclusion allows us to affirm the inalienable dignity of a human life, the tension at its heart cautions against a dogmatism that dictates to people how they should live.

Bishops, therefore, who insist on upholding a rigid and loveless orthodoxy are little emperors strutting about in public with no clothes. Their leadership has more to do with the controlling spirit of Empire than with the loving spirit of Christ. I should perhaps qualify this judgement in the case of some African Christian leaders, who have had only modest educational opportunities and for whom the martyrs of Buganda, killed for resisting a homosexual tyrant, are a relatively recent memory. An inflexible approach to Christian tradition is also to some extent understandable in those who have suffered at the hands of monstrous evil. The Nazi occupation of Poland in World War II, followed by communist totalitarianism, clearly left Pope John Paul II, for one, with a very black and white view of the world, and with the determination to hold catholic tradition all along the line as the only sure defence against barbarism.

However, one cannot afford to be too generous to one's fundamentalist opponents – even as big a celebrity as was the Polish Pope – because it would be utterly foolish to follow them in a world that seldom presents us with moral dilemmas that are black and white. To draw all this back to the personal, it is sobering to think that had Alison and I followed papal teaching on contraception, for instance, we would by now likely have a tribe of underfed, scruffy and, because it would not have been possible to give them individual attention, delinquent children. The strain of it all on our marriage would be almost unthinkable. Alison would certainly never have fulfilled her vocation as a doctor and been able to care for the homeless and prisoners. Going further back into my past, instead of taking the train to my safe single-sex boarding school in Natal, had I boarded 'The Train to Johannesburg' from Teyateyaneng with only the Pope's condemnation of condoms ringing in my ears, I would now be dead – along with scores of my generation of BaSotho mineworkers and their wives and children. And all for the sake of the obscure Christian tradition that insists every sexual act include the possibility of procreation.

If Alison and my lives and those of innumerable ordinary people count for anything in the great scheme of things, it is therefore very important that we resist religious nonsense in those who should know better and challenge those who, for whatever understandable reason, mistakenly cling to traditional certainties. Fortunately modern Europeans, while they may briefly turn out in their millions to mourn a Christian celebrity, do not take dogmatic religious leaders seriously. It is also heartening that though the people have moved on from the Church they have not entirely lost touch with faith and morals. A good illustration of this is the way secular European society, both applying and developing our Christian understanding of the human person as being made in the image of God, insists on including the homosexual in a universal theory of human rights. It will not be the first time that the Church has had to show some humility and revise its tradition accordingly.

Finally, to address the thorny issue of Christian unity, if, in developing the tradition to include practising homosexual clergy and women bishops, the Church of England and the Anglican Communion should distance itself even further from Rome and break up, sad as that will be, so be it. While any loosening of the bonds of affection between Christians is to be regretted, a good clean break may even be a good thing in so far as Anglican churches outside England would be forced to work more closely with their ecumenical partners to develop a more indigenous Christianity. They are, after all, the product of an empire that has ceased to exist and, in any case, most of them are ignorant of the Reformation disputes and power struggles that formed the Church of England. Why, therefore, perpetuate structures that keep local Christians apart?

And back home in England, a good clean break would release Anglicans into a closer engagement with modern, secular and multi-faith Britain and a post-9/11 world, where the stakes are so high we cannot simply go on as before. This is the rainbow world God has called us to make peace in; there is no other. And if it has become impossible to sustain with fellow Christians the distinctive Anglican way of being the church, where we agree to belong, rather than belong to agree, then why not explore this way of being a human community with other people of goodwill in friendship circles? Is this not the direction our Anglican tradition has been pointing in for some time, but which we have feared to follow because it will mean the end of the Church of England as we know it? And could it be that, in dying to self, the Church of England will lead on towards the future of Christianity and of Faith?

My answer to each of these questions must be an expectant and definite yes. As I look back on my life's journey thus far, in the course of which I have lived through the end of Britain's African Empire, the end of White supremacy in South Africa, the end of orthodox Christianity (whatever that was) and now all the signs that the Church of England is gradually slowing to a full stop, I find that I am no longer surprised by the ending of things. Trying to make sense of all these closures, what is so hopeful is that empires, churches and even world religions eventually give way to fresh movements of the human spirit. Whatever the future, it is vital we resist the desperate violence of the passing order and allow love to beckon us on and into a larger sense of belonging to the one human family, with all its glorious diversity.

INDEX